Talking about Jesus Today

An Introduction to the Story
Behind Our Faith

William Reiser, S.J.

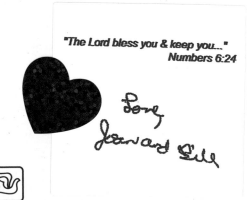

"The Lord bless you & keep you..."
Numbers 6:24

Love
Leonard Bill

PAULIST PRESS
New York and Mahwah, N.J.

IMPRIMI POTEST:
Very Rev. William A. Barry, S.J.
Provincial
Society of Jesus of New England

Library of Congress Cataloging-in-Publication Data

Reiser, William E.
   Talking about Jesus today : an introduction to the story behind
our faith / William Reiser.
     p. cm.
   Includes bibliographical references.
   ISBN 0-8091-3358-X (pbk.)
   1. Jesus Christ—Person and offices. 2. Jesus Christ—Biography.
I. Title.
BT205.R358   1993
232'.8—dc20   92-33240
                                       CIP

Published by Paulist Press
997 Macarthur Boulevard
Mahwah, NJ 07430

Printed and bound in the
United States of America

Contents

PART THREE: WHO IS JESUS?

PART FOUR: THE LAST DAYS

PART FIVE: NEWNESS OF LIFE

ACKNOWLEDGEMENT

This book comes out of my life in the Society of Jesus, whose Spanish name *La Compañía de Jesús* beautifully carries the ring of being-with-Jesus: the company or companions of Jesus. Without the special urging of Father Gerald O'Collins and Robert White, I would not be teaching theology today. Without the warm fraternal encouragement of Fathers Robert Manning and Paul Harman, I would not be writing about Jesus. Without the friendship, openness and gracious hospitality of Father Francisco Pifarré and the Bolivian Jesuit scholastics at Casa Pedro Arrupe in Cochabamba, the wonderful desires from which springs the theology of liberation would have remained for me faceless and abstract. And without the Jesuit Community at Holy Cross College, I might never have appreciated how much the Society means to me.

A Word to the Student Reader

This book has been written with you in mind; it is the product of someone who teaches theology at the undergraduate level in a Catholic liberal arts college. Often when a person writes, he carries on an imaginary conversation with some particular audience, and what generally was in my mind's eye as I wrote these pages was the faces of students I have had the privilege of teaching over a number of semesters: their questions, their interests, their intellectual religious needs, and their faith. On occasion (rare, I hope) I may have slipped into imagining another audience, too, namely, other teachers. This was probably inevitable. It is important to me that, if any teachers should read this, they should know what lies behind my adopting a particular perspective. Thus, there is some information included in the text which is equivalently footnote material, and the bibliography at the end affords some idea of what sources I have been drawing upon.

Yet my primary concern has been for the students, whether undergraduates like the ones in my classroom, or those who have already finished their college studies and have retained an interest in theological reflection. As young Christian adults, you have many healthy questions about what your religious tradition teaches and about what you are required to hold today (which is probably not always the same thing as what you really believe). From my viewpoint as a teacher, however, what truly matters most is the story of Jesus, because, more than the church, or our parents, or our teachers, that story is what really controls our grasp of the beliefs which count experientially. What has bothered me is that far too many Christians are not deeply familiar with that story. All of us have listened to the gospel readings on Sundays over a number of years, and thus we know the story in bits and pieces. Those pieces have been loosely stitched together by what I would call a mythologized picture of Jesus as the humble yet almighty Son of God: the Son of man who works miracles and expels demons, who summons men and women so authoritatively that they follow him immediately and unquestioningly, who walks upon stormy seas and multiplies loaves and fishes, who wrestles with Satan himself in the desert and ultimately lays down his life out of love, for the sins of the human race. In some respects, this Jesus is like us; in many respects, he is not.

Each one of us needs to get inside the gospel story so that it roots itself in our imaginations, stirs our desires, rearranges our loyalties. The only way to verify for oneself that Jesus is of God is to live the gospel. Jesus is all the church claims he is, and more, yet the way the story has been imparted has not always been faithful to the memory of Jesus. There is something dangerous and subversive about the gospel story: the very same thing which makes it good news to the poor causes it to be very unsettling news for those who are well off. Jesus was not crucified, after all, for teaching catechism to children and unlettered peasants. Even for the church itself, which always stands under the gospel, the memory of Jesus can be a painful corrective when it either loses its nerve or fudges the prophetic message it should be both preaching and practicing.

Over the centuries, the Christian tradition has laid transparencies across the story of Jesus. He becomes more majestic, more divine, more privatized, and less historical. If we could pull back some of those transparencies, we would find ourselves in touch with a different Jesus. No one in his or her right mind could reject the glorified Lord, if Jesus were suddenly to appear before us the way he reportedly did to Saint Paul on the Damascus road (see Acts 9). But people could very well reject the Jesus who stood face-to-face with the scribes and Pharisees, the prostitutes and tax-collectors, and all the other gospel characters. They had a choice to make with respect to Jesus, and many of them chose to reject him. However risky it sounds, we need to be in that position, too, in order to hear the radical demands which Jesus makes. The rich young person of the gospel story could be any one of us. At the moment when Jesus told him what he had to do "if you wish to be perfect," his face fell and he walked away (Mt 19:16–22). I have never found a young person who did not wish to be perfect, but I have encountered plenty who want to determine for themselves what perfection means. As I said, we would find it well-nigh impossible to walk away from a Jesus who was fully revealed to us in all his glory. Yet this is never the sort of revelation which is given. In fact, any expectation of such self-disclosure by Jesus is bound to leave us frustrated, because it completely overlooks what faith is all about. In God's providence, faith is what brings the process of our becoming human to fulfillment.

According to the gospel story, some people actually did walk away from Jesus, and they continue to do so, since the Jesus they have learned about is not the real Jesus. One does not have to take a mythologized Jesus seriously, because, like a pious statue, a mythologized Jesus never really sets foot in human history. A mythologized Jesus never actually intercepts us. Our paths never cross. But the Jesus of the gospel story is something else. For better or worse, he meets us through the retelling of the gospel story, and in that instant when we look at him face-to-face, our very lives hang in the balance.

The intention behind this book is simple. It is intended to assist you to walk through selected moments in the story of Jesus in order to discover what Christian faith is built on. It makes no pretensions about raising all the relevant questions, and it is not a full-scale contemporary "life of Christ" (for reasons which should become clear in the Introduction). Although the book does not develop reflections on all the major gospel scenes, it assumes that the study of Jesus begins with careful, close reading of the gospels themselves. Some passages need to be read and pondered many times before one starts to get a feel for what Jesus truly stood for. The study of Jesus proceeds more fruitfully if the person is also talking with other believers about their experience of faith. It proceeds best if one has the advantage of sound spiritual direction. Theological reflection starts when believing people have questions about what they believe and why they believe it; but the activity of reflection builds upon a living faith. Thus, the spiritual and the academic, what feeds the soul and what feeds the mind, have to blend together. Scholarship without faith is sterile; faith without scholarship is naive and in danger of being a hostage to reason.

Early in the gospel story, Jesus reacts to those who are having trouble accepting him and his message by saying that new wine demands new wineskins, for old wineskins are too brittle to stretch under the fermenting action of the freshly pressed grapes (Mk 2:22). The same point holds true with respect to our understanding of Jesus. Sometimes we cannot hear what the gospel story is telling us because the images, ideas and concepts with which we approach it are too brittle or tight; we miss discovering who Jesus really is because our minds have been shut to anything new. We incline, instead, toward the conventional Jesus who does little more than ask us to lead morally decent lives. Whenever this shrinkage occurs, we need someone to help us see what is going on. Changing our mental wineskins may prove painful; conversion seldom proceeds without some discomfort as our heads readjust to the fermenting action of grace.

One depends upon teachers, too, for the gospels are ancient texts. Frequently the meaning of those texts will not be exposed apart from hard, serious scholarship. But this point should hardly be surprising. Any of you who have studied classical literature has learned that it would be very easy to miss what a text is saying if the reader has little idea of its historical background, the allusions it makes, its initial audience, and so forth. The more insight one has into the times of Jesus, as well as into the situations out of which the evangelists composed their narratives, the more fruitful (and enjoyable) will be one's reading of the gospel story. Again, that is why the Christian community needs both scholars and teachers.

Still, there should be nothing daunting about reading the gospels, as if one needs to know everything before one can start. After all, a person has to begin somewhere. Even after fifteen years of teaching, at times I feel like a hiker making his way through a swamp where I am not always sure whether what I am about to step on is a rock or a submerged crocodile. The study of scripture alone, not to mention the study of the later Christian tradition, could exhaust several lifetimes. Yet we only have one lifetime, and needless to say, we also have to get about the business of living. A teacher has to trust that whatever is not covered during the course may be discovered elsewhere, and that whatever mistakes he has unwittingly made will one day be corrected by someone else, or by God's grace working through a person's own experience.

As a way of approaching the pages that follow, you might pose this question to yourself: "Who is Jesus for me?" This basic question should orient us to look not only at what we think about Jesus, but also at what our experience of Jesus has been. And then to test how much weight that answer carries, you might pose the further question: "What would I be prepared to do as a consequence of who he is for me?" An even sharper way to frame this might be to ask, "What can I envision myself doing *with Jesus* for the sake of the kingdom of God?" There are many things we might be prepared to do *for* Jesus on the basis of our preconceived ideas about who he is, for who could say "No" to the Son of God? But for someone entering the world of the gospel story, it might make more sense to think about what we would be willing to do *together with Jesus,* because that was the situation in which the disciples found themselves. This might help us to appraise who we truly think Jesus is more realistically. The answer to the second question thus creates the possibility of answering the first.

In order to answer the first question ("Who is Jesus for me?"), we need to know something of the gospel story, because that is where the memories about Jesus have been preserved. To answer the second question, we first need to know something about what Jesus actually did (and not only what he taught), since Jesus can expect nothing of his disciples which he has not done himself. A famous and spiritually influential work from the fifteenth century entitled *The Imitation of Christ* inspired countless men and women to imitate the virtues and interior dispositions of Jesus. Many of us in an older generation used to read from it faithfully each week. But the Jesus of *The Imitation of Christ* had a monastic transparency laid over him. He appeared serene and timeless, a model of perfection to be emulated.

Jesus, however, was more than a teacher and exemplar of virtue. The imitation of Christ in our day is going to take us through a very different route. It will conduct us through the heart of the world and its historical experience, especially through the hopes and the anxieties, the joys and the fears of those who have been marginalized as a result of poverty, unemployment, lack of education, illness, old age, repressive political systems, racial and ethnic discrimination. The imitation of Christ today necessarily involves us in the human struggle for justice; that is going to be the result of one's encounter with the faith of Jesus. There are two questions, then: "Who is Jesus?" and "What am I prepared to do as a result of this answer?" I should add that these two questions only make sense if one is already inside the believing community. For those who are on the outside, the questions will be quite different. I suspect that they would be asking, "What is the Christian community?" And, "What makes that community live and behave the way it does?" As far as this book is concerned, I am addressing myself to people like you, for whom talking about Jesus is already important.

It might be worth remembering that whatever we know about

Jesus has come to us by way of the faith and example of his followers from one age to the next, and whatever those who follow us may come to understand about the story will depend a great deal upon what we profess and what witness we give. The more open we are to hearing the gospel story in order to enter it and live it, the more we are going to understand Jesus. The more distractedly we hear the story, because of "worldly anxiety, the lure of riches, and the craving for other things" (Mk 4:19), the more our understanding of Jesus is going to be choked.

One last word before we start. In the Introduction I have tried to convey some sense of the voice behind these pages and its affection for the subject matter. It is also important to give a little background on what might be called the "book behind the book," which for me was one of those grateful discoveries a person makes in life now and then.

Introduction

About ten years ago, a Jesuit friend of mine who has been working as a missioner in the mountain villages of Honduras urged me to get my hands on a copy of a book entitled *Un tal Jesus*, a creative retelling of the gospel story for the people of Latin America. I chanced upon it during the summer of 1989 while studying at the Maryknoll Language Institute in Cochabamba. My friend's enthusiasm proved to be more than justified. *Un tal Jesus* blended together Christology, contemporary New Testament studies and liberation theology in a way that highlighted, skillfully yet simply, both the immensely attractive humanness of Jesus and the overarching divine commitment to liberating human beings from every form of oppression. Since the time I finished graduate studies in 1977, the only other work to have left such an indelible imprint on my mind was James Dunn's *Jesus and the Spirit*. Dunn's study carefully sifted through the New Testament texts in order to uncover the basic elements of Jesus' religious experience. If Jesus was fully human, then he obviously had to have religious or faith experience, just as we do; and whatever light could be shed on that experience of his would illumine both his humanity and ours. *Jesus and the Spirit* was absolutely refreshing, but it was undoubtedly too academic a work for the average reader.

For a number of years I had been toying with the idea of writing a life of Christ. I recall that in 1962, during my second year of college, I had followed up on the earnest recommendation of the butcher in our neighborhood grocery store and read Romano Guardini's *The Lord* (1954). This was a book whose meditative, existential approach to the various episodes of Jesus' life opened up for me an intellectually and spiritually invigorating way to appropriate the gospels. A year or so later, in the Jesuit novitiate, my imagination would be deeply and wonderfully captured by Alban Goodier's two-volume work *The Public Life of our Lord Jesus Christ* (1931). These two works had long been serving as the mental parameters for the book I had been contemplating; but I had learned enough about the nature of the gospels to realize that devotional lives of Christ, which had been so popular among several generations of Catholic readers, could never again succeed. The evangelists had simply failed to provide sufficient material for a coherent and sustained presentation of Jesus' life. Rather, the gospels drew us into contact with the faith of a number of early Christian communities, and, indirectly, they also brought us into close proximity with the faith and human experience of Jesus. The prospect of a contemporary life of Christ which might inspire and challenge a new generation of readers, along the lines of a Goodier or a Guardini, but which kept Jesus' faith and human experience rather than his divinity as its point of reference, seemed to be ever more remote. However interesting to read, Nikos Kazantzakis' *The Last Temptation of Christ* (1960) had proven to me that, while a life of Christ could be imaginative, it could not afford to be fiction.

I admit to being a Christian by imagination and feeling, more than by logic and reason. I did pass through a phase in the middle of my theology studies when I thought I had outgrown my fascination with the gospel as story and discovered the adult side of Christian faith. The gospels of Mark, Luke and Matthew interested me less and less, and I was turning with relish to John and the letters of Paul. In them, I believed, I had found a grown-up expression of the Christian mystery, for, on the basis of long contemplation of the death and resurrection of Jesus they had explicated the great theological truths which formed our religion. Believers unschooled in the intricacies of faith would continue to listen to and imaginatively live in the story; those more advanced would not want milk, but the substantial intellectual nourishment of Paul and John. I wince when I recall that stage now. As Joseph Appleyard explains in the last chapter of his book *Becoming a Reader*, the truly adult reader (and, I would add, the truly adult believer) need make no apology for reading what satisfies the cravings of imagination. We live, after all, out of our feelings as much as out of our ideas, and besides, the ideas which truly matter to us are ideas which we feel strongly about. Imagination is often the way by which ideas acquire their feel. My intellectual awkwardness with the gospel as story was, in retrospect, both adolescent and mercifully temporary. The human soul naturally inclines more toward story than to metaphysics, because story, like the needle of a compass, points our minds in the direction of life and our hearts in the direction of truth. At least, this has been my experience.

At any rate, it was against such a background that my imagination finally landed upon *Un tal Jesus: La buena noticia contada al pueblo de América Latina*, which might be translated, "A Certain Jesus: The good news as told to the people of Latin America." Written by a brother and sister team, José Ignacio and María López Vigil, both veteran laborers among Latin American Christian communities, the work (or, more precisely, the script of 144 radio programs) was published in Salamanca in 1982. [I was informed that some members of the Latin American Episcopal Conference, which had taken a conservative turn in the years since their breathtaking Assemblies at Medellín (1968) and Puebla (1979), had been endeavoring to suppress the tapes of those broadcasts.] This was the book, I soon realized, which I had secretly been wanting to write all along. "That's the way it actually was!" I kept exclaiming to myself as I made my way, chapter by chapter, through this version of the gospel story. For reasons I cannot altogether account for, I had the queer yet firm recollection of having been "there" before, as if, after two thousand years of lapsed memory, I had somehow awakened to the startling realization that I had been present to these scenes and events centuries ago. The work so excited me that it was all I could think or talk about for several months afterwards. The first time I devoted a seminar to *Un tal Jesus* the students did not want to see the course come to an end.

The theology of *Un tal Jesus* arises out of the experience of men and women fighting to surmount enormous poverty, economic exploitation and political violence. The story "works" by drawing a parallel between the situation of injustice in many parts of Central and South America today and the life and time of Jesus. Jesus becomes a *campesino* whose awareness of himself as a prophet grows and develops, whose basic message is about the kingdom of God being a kingdom of justice, whose humanity is never eclipsed by divinity, and whose good news is as much the attractiveness of his own personality and humanity as it is the message about God's kingdom. He tells jokes and stories. He sings and dances. His hands are calloused from hard work, and, like so many in South America, he even has a nickname, "*Moreno*," "the dark one," because of the color of his skin.

There were two things which my students enjoyed about the book. First, they fell in love with the figure of Jesus. From week to week, they would remark about how human Jesus appeared there, so unlike the portrait of him they had grown up with. His story assumed a kind of naturalness, indeed, a believability, which drew them into the gospel. They would never again be able to read or hear many gospel passages the same way as before. *Un tal Jesus* had made the gospel story come alive without reducing it to the genre of religious fantasy. Jesus had feelings and emotions, as did his companions, and his mother. He lived and breathed in this world. However prophetically he would react to the things he witnessed, Jesus never came across as mysterious, other-worldly, or serenely ascetical. Even the Jesus who was raised from the dead still remained the companion and friend; he had not suddenly become a distant, elevated supernatural being. The book had helped some of them to relate to Jesus, really and earnestly, for the first time. For the first time, they heard a Jesus who laughed.

The second thing the students liked about the book was the way it deployed the theme of justice and God's "preferential love for the poor" throughout Jesus' ministry. For, just as the figure of Jesus as they knew it had seemed remote and unreal, so too his mission and work seemed unconnected with the pressing concerns of ordinary men and women. The Jesus they had been raised with was completely divorced from history, more a citizen of heaven than of the earth. He was a model of moral behavior, a teacher of high spiritual ideals and values, their point of contact with the unseen God, and the one who had rescued them in some inexplicable fashion from their sins. In fact, their understanding of salvation and redemption was so focussed on the remission of sin and eternal life that the good news about Jesus himself amounted to little more than a pious curiosity or a soothing tale for world-weary souls; it had as much relevance as a statue of the Infant of Prague.

To put the matter bluntly, *Un tal Jesus* had given the story of Jesus back its guts. There really was something worth proclaiming and worth laboring to help men and women understand. There really was a "divine cause" which Jesus had taken upon his shoulders upon being baptized at the Jordan. The gospel, fully lived, could make a difference to history, not merely in the private space of the individual's own spiritual development but in the public space of communities, politics and society, and culture. The matter of human sinfulness, which ultimately came to account theologically for why Jesus was crucified, was absolutely inseparable from the concrete misery, powerlessness and injustice that had caused the prophetic voices of old to blaze out against the rich and powerful of the land; the same evils would have stirred the soul of Jesus.

Many people find it difficult to comprehend why the church, in talking about Jesus, makes so much of sin when forgiveness comes so easily. And the reason for their bewilderment is that the forgiveness of sins is not so much a matter of sacrament and ritual as it is a matter of doing justice and promoting reconciliation among men and women. The real work of redemption, in other words, involves throwing oneself, heart and soul, into confronting and transforming all the forces, structures, relationships and institutions which rob human beings of their freedom and suck away their life. This task is something to which we can devote our lives, too, just as Jesus did. His story has a compelling reason for being retold.

The reader comes away from *Un tal Jesus*, then, with two graces which have worked one over intellectually and morally. One discovers a new way of relating to "a certain person named Jesus" and one senses that the real purpose of Jesus' life was both more complex and more exciting than the claim that he came to take away the sins of the world generally sounds. Furthermore, these graces suggest two focal points for talking about Jesus today. Jesus was fully and attractively human, more so, perhaps, than any of us might ever hope to be; and God had chosen the side of those who counted as nothing in the eyes of the world: those chronically hungry, those who thirsted for righteousness and justice, those whose basic rights had been violated, those burdened by poverty, guilt and sin. What is there left for us to do, except to want to be with Jesus and to continue doing what he has begun?

In addition to the seminar, I also teach a course entitled "Understanding Jesus." There, as a starting point for talking about Jesus, I choose the gospel of Mark both because his is the earliest gospel we have and because Matthew and Luke enjoyed the advantage of reading Mark before they wrote. In a semester with thirteen weeks of class, it has not been uncommon for me to reach the end of the tenth week and still be charting a path through Mark's telling of the story of Jesus, despite my more ambitious goal of surveying the Christologies of the other gospels, Paul, and the classic doctrines of the fourth and fifth centuries! The more I teach the course, the less ground we seem to cover. At first, I thought that the reason for this was that I kept having to fill in gaps left by previous catechetical instruction, and the truth is that students today arrive at college knowing increasingly less about their faith. But then I began to suspect that another reason was at work which kept slowing me down and preventing me from "covering the matter," as the older Jesuits used to say.

Most students generally have more questions about their religious beliefs than anyone could reasonably answer in a single semester. Frequently these questions are purely informational. But one morning, after responding to all of the class' questions, I noticed that a number of faces still appeared dissatisfied. All at once it dawned on me that the basic difficulty never really was over this or that particular aspect of Christian belief. Rather, the uneasiness arose from the fact that a faulty version of the gospel story had been steadily playing in the background, like a silent video. Whatever they heard in class was being accepted or rejected, depending upon whether it conformed to the perspective of that presentation of the story of Jesus which was playing in the recesses of their minds.

The underlying problem in talking about Jesus today is often not about specific teachings, such as original sin, or the virginal conception of Jesus, or even the divinity of Christ; it is about the underlying story. The reason why many people do not hear what the gospel may be saying about Jesus is that it does not square with their inner video. The camera of their imaginations has been fixed on a very different version of the story. What I learned from all of this was that the teacher first and foremost had to be a storyteller. Ever so carefully and respectfully, one has to lift off the old video and replace it with something new. Fresh wine, after all, demands fresh wineskins.

The real reason, therefore, that the course was staying longer with the gospel of Mark was that we needed to spend more time with the story itself. The course was covering less of the subject matter which I had staked out and more of the matter which the students themselves had been staking out, without realizing it. They wanted to hear the story of Jesus, which meant that the teacher had to learn how to tell it. The teacher had to become a storyteller. But like young people everywhere, my students were also quick to pick up whether the storyteller was sincere, or merely pretending for the sake of effect. Just as the homilist cannot preach what he does not live, so too the one who would tell Jesus' story cannot narrate what he or she has not in some way witnessed.

The stories we tell best are the ones of which we have been a part. In retelling the story of Jesus, therefore, those tell it best for whom his story has somehow become theirs. Yet, is it not to some extent true that for every believer, the history beneath the Jesus story, which is the history to which we have been present through imagination, may have to remain permanently concealed, because that history has been so intricately pieced into one's own life? Might we not have to declare, in all frankness and honesty, that we can no longer disentangle Jesus' story from our own, that we cannot talk about ourselves without speaking about him? Faith, after all, is much more than an ideological super-structure mounted on top of one's "real" life; the mystery of God is not an optional "extra" to human living. The mystery of God, and the faith which brings that mystery to awareness in our minds and hearts, is the soul's inner dynamic, woven into the very center of human existence, providing us with our deepest identity; pull away from God and that identity unravels. This, of course, was how it was with Jesus. Apart from the mystery of God, Jesus would be absolutely unintelligible.

The same holds true for the community of his disciples. Apart from the Spirit of Jesus, the Christian community—its values, its witness, its missionary outreach, its passion for justice, its fidelity to one another, its manner of living—would make absolutely no sense. Pull away from Jesus, and the community's identity unravels, too. Who then is Jesus? What are we prepared to undertake with Jesus because we, like him, have trusted that God will keep the divine promise to set the world free? These are the questions which will guide our walking through the gospel story.

PART ONE:
BACKGROUND

1

Preparing To Hear the Story

If we had been Christians of the first century who wanted either to meditate upon or to share with others the story of Jesus, one of the most natural things in the world to do would have been to comb through the Hebrew scriptures, or what the church later came to refer to as the "Old" Testament. There, in the pages of the historical books which chronicled the development of the relationship between God and the people of Israel, in the verses of the great prayer book which was the Book of Psalms, in the energy and passion of the prophetic works, in the faith-filled ponderings of the wisdom literature, in the wonderfully revealing chapters of the creation story, in the subversive memory of Israel's miraculous deliverance from slavery in Egypt within the Book of Exodus, and in the twin treasures of God's law and God's promise from the Book of Deuteronomy, we find the roots of Jesus' historical and cultural identity, his convictions about God, and the great national hopes which he had inherited. The early communities turned warmly and often to these scriptures in order to understand better the Jesus who had become the center of their own relationship with God. Not only will the evangelists, and Paul, for example, cite passages from the Old Testament; they frequently assume that their readers are familiar with those texts, too. The church eventually came to make the Hebrew scriptures its own, since apart from them Jesus would have no history, no ancestors, indeed, no humanity. Perhaps that helps to explain why Matthew and Luke trace the ancestry of Jesus back through David and Abraham (Mt 1:1), and through Adam to God (Lk 3:38). Without a genealogy, and without all the history that a genealogy contains, Jesus would not have been someone of flesh and blood.

In order to find out where Jesus is coming from, we need to know the key portions of this literature. We need to sit a while with the early chapters of Genesis, for example, in order to steep our imaginations in the creation story and let its lessons sink in: that the world and all that is in it comes from God; that human life is sacred, since we are fashioned in the divine image and likeness; that disorder arose when human beings, as a result of their disobedience, fell victim to fear, and that when fear entered the world it gave death its power; that God makes promises and remains active in human history, because God ever remains our Creator. We need to acquire some sense of Israel's history and experience of oppression, from the years in Egypt to the exile in Babylon, and savor the belief that the God of Israel is a politically liberating God who remains faithful to what has been divinely promised. We need, too, to listen to the voices of the prophets, who clamor for justice and champion the cause of the poor and defenseless people of the land, since among the prophets God's love is decidedly "preferential." And, finally, we have to look to the Psalms, because there we will find the religious experience of Israel and Israel's fundamental religious intuitions about divine faithfulness, compassion and goodness. There we will discover the array of feelings which accompanied Israel's special relationship with God, and we will notice the freedom in which Israel approached God and poured out its soul, sometimes in anger, sometimes in sorrow, sometimes in disappointment, sometimes in praise. For God, the people knew, always listens and, in one way or another, always responds. The God of Israel was personal; God had a name, and a heart.

Most readers have no conceptual difficulties with all of this. Their questions arise in connection with various details in some of the stories. Was there really a garden? Doesn't God appear rather petty and inept? After all, didn't he know what sort of creatures he had made, that they would disobey and turn to sin? God seems to be angry a great deal, always dissatisfied with human beings and chastising them. The conception of God in the early chapters of the Bible appears irritatingly anthropomorphic. Once this is explained, however, readers are ready to move along, provided, of course, that they do not have to subscribe to this primitive biblical picture of God. Oddly enough, however, the idea of God many of us carry is also quite anthropomorphic, minus the temper tantrums. Our understanding of what God is like has frequently still to be challenged and corrected by Jesus' experience of God. But one cannot address every question at once. Many of them will be resolved quietly, as the gospel story is retold.

Divine Promise: A Thematic Unity between the Old and New Testaments

Let me add three comments by way of postscript. First, although it is understandable how ordinary believers could form the impression that the God of the Old Testament was something of a crab at times, while the God of the New Testament was patient and merciful, this perception hardly does justice to the facts. It oversimplifies too much of the Bible. The face of God is often full of compassion and love in the Old, and the God of the New is on occasion depicted very sternly. What may be more to the point, however, is the contrast between an historically involved God and a somewhat more spiritual or celestial one. The God of the Old gets his hands dirty, as it were, in his constant preoccupation with a stiff-necked people; the God of the New remains quietly above things, content to let the drama unfold through the life of Jesus. What the alert reader frequently detects is the shift from divine saving activity within history, to redemptive activity above and beyond history. The Old tells the story of God's actions within this world; the New has its eye on the new Jerusalem beyond this world.

It is good to single out this perception early and deal with it, because, although it more closely diagnoses the discomfort some Christians have with the Old Testament, it overlooks the fact that the same God who acts in the ministry of Jesus acted through the prophets of old. What links the Old and the New is the continuity of divine promise and divine saving (or creative) action in and through history. Such thematic continuity lies, for example, at the core of the transfiguration episode recounted in the gospels, where Jesus entered into conversation with Moses and Elijah, and the approving voice of God suddenly thundered through the cloud (Mk 9:2–8). For the evangelists, there had been no rupture or failure in continuity between what had been and what is taking place now; the plane on which the historically revealing God of Israel had operated in the past would be the same plane in the future. Only the geography would change, for the God of

Israel was at the same time the God of all nations, as Paul reminds us in his letter to the Romans (Rom 3:29–30).

The Secular Word of God

Secondly, while scripture is clearly the major text for reflecting upon the person of Jesus today, there is a second major text, which for me has been *The New York Times*. Once in a while I have found myself musing that, if I were a bishop, I would tell the clergy of my diocese that they could consider the *Times* as part of the Office of Readings. Not a day goes by when there is not something in the paper that bears upon the sorry state of our human condition. There are stories about human beings done in by their own greed, or about people consumed by the desire for power. We read about the struggle of people for freedom and independence, about the thirst for justice and democratic government. We learn about tyrannies, and the deadly human assault upon the earth's environment, corporate cover-ups and governmental refusals to promote the common good. Peasants in Colombia or Guatemala are massacred by death squads in the pay of wealthy landowners, human beings by the thousands have their lives wrecked by alcohol and drug addiction, street children in Brazil or South Africa are killed by men who consider them a public nuisance, and young girls in New York City have to join street gangs for protection against the violence around them. From every part of the world one hears the groaning for liberty, for food, for education, health care and decent housing, for an end to repression, for deliverance from addictions.

Each day the human story unfolds a little more, and in that story the attentive reader discerns the background which would give rise to the human cry for justice, to profound hope, to the soul-wrenching faith that God has not abandoned the world. Obviously, there is more to the news than the tale of human tragedy and grief, and to the recounting of human sinfulness. Yet, nevertheless, there the human condition is chronicled in all its bloody detail like a modern-day scripture. To understand the background of the Jesus story, one needs the Old Testament, to be sure. One needs some familiarity with the historical and cultural circumstances of his life and times as well. In addition, however, one has to feel the throbbing cries of desperate human beings for deliverance in order to grasp the gospel's central message. Until such conversion of sympathies occurs, one is not ready to study the story of Jesus. To anyone who would object that it is frivolous to suggest any comparison between a newspaper and sacred scripture, I would answer along the lines of Nicholas Lash that "it is not the case that all experience of God is necessarily religious in form or content, and that not everything which it would be appropriate to characterize as 'religious' experience would thereby necessarily constitute experience of God" (*Easter in Ordinary* [Charlottesville: University Press of Virginia, 1988], p. 289). Nothing prevents the "word of God" from reaching us through the most "ordinary" of texts.

Can Christian Belief Be Tested?

Thirdly, it is taken for granted that students enrolled in a biology or chemistry course will have to take a laboratory class, too. All of them understand the role and importance of "labs" in science courses. That is where theory is tested and students grasp the ancient idea that science is born out of invention, discovery or experience. Yet why should the same not hold for theology courses? What about the "theory" upon which the study of God is founded, namely, that the holy mystery of God has entered into conversation with human beings? The laboratory component of a theology course, therefore, would be spiritual direction, since it is usually in the context of spiritual direction that believing men and women have the opportunity to learn how to notice and clarify their experience of God. Sometimes this is done individually with the assistance of an experienced guide or director, at other times it takes place in a group setting: in either case, the "direction" consists in helping someone attend to the presence and action of God in his or her life.

If God is truly at work in the world and within human history, it should strike no one as surprising that the mystery of God is also at work in one's own life. But do I really know this? Have I observed and reflected upon it? Through one's own experience, the great theological intuitions about God can be confirmed. God is the Creator. God both makes promises and keeps them, that is, God is faithful. God works within history, to create, to heal, to redeem and forgive, to liberate from every kind of oppression. God is good, and God loves, compassionately and freely, each and every one of us. The most basic truths are always "spiritual": and if they are truly for the human spirit, they can in principle be confirmed by experience. Prayer and spiritual direction help to keep our experience from becoming illegible.

Theology without spiritual direction lacks a vital ingredient. For if theological reflection is purely a matter of the head thinking without the heart praying, then it does not bring people closer to the divine mystery. In which case, one rightly asks, why take a theology course? One would do better taking a class in the study of religion. The point may be medieval, even older, but it is still sound and well worth repeating at the outset.

2

The Pattern of a People's Experience

There are at least four elements to what might be called the pattern of Israel's religious experience. These elements pertain not only to the way that Jesus lived and thought, but also to the attitude or disposition with which we as listeners approach his story: creation, promise, prayer and prophecy. We understand Jesus better to the degree that we have internalized the great biblical truths which constituted his religious outlook on the world.

1. The Experience of Creation

Creation refers to the lived realization that each person is absolutely dependent upon God; that the earth belongs to the Lord and thus deserves to be treated with the utmost courtesy; that the divine image and likeness, according to which we have been fashioned, may be blurred, but it can never be erased; and that, finally, all that we have is pure gift. These are the essential truths of the creation myth in the Book of Genesis. As truths, they have to be personally appropriated through meditation and periodic retelling of the creation story, and then expressed through one's day-to-day engagement with the world. These four truths are foundational intuitions; they ground us in reality (to some degree they even create reality for us) and they help constitute our identity. Indeed, they determine the way we define ourselves and our place in the universe.

2. Faith in the Divine Promise

Promise refers to the fact that the God of Israel's experience has not only created the past (the way things were at the beginning), but also creates the future (the way things will be at the end). In fact, the memory of how things once stood between God and human beings in the garden is at the same time an expression of human hope for the future: a vision of human community and oneness with the earth which is sustained by the great gift of intimacy with the Creator himself. The promise of God opens up the possibility of a future moment when Israel, and all the nations of the earth, will be fully liberated from every form of oppression.

The condition for realizing the divine promise is faithfulness on the part of the people to that other gift from God, namely, the Law. Obedience to the Law meant following the way of life, which was the way of God (Deut 30:15–20). With respect to the statutes and decrees he had passed on from the Lord, Moses instructed the people of Israel:

> Observe them carefully, for thus will you give evidence of your wisdom and intelligence to the nations, who will hear of all these statutes and say, "This great nation is truly a wise and intelligent people." For what great nation is there that has gods so close to it as the Lord, our God, is to us whenever we call upon him? Or what great nation has statutes and decrees that are as just as this whole law which I am setting before you today? (Deut 4:6–8)

Promise is an historical category: the God who makes promises is a God who has become involved in human affairs, creating the very future which he himself revealed. But the correlative of promise is loyalty and faith, which are expressed in terms of obedience and hope.

3. Experiencing God in Prayer

The third element running through Israel's pattern of religious experience is *prayer*, or more exactly, it is *Israel's experience of God as expressed in its prayer*. Nowhere else does Israel's faith come to such full expression as in the Psalms. There all the different moments of its historical experience are recapitulated, from the experience of being created, of being called and specially chosen, of being blessed, of being chastised, and of being abandoned to the nation's enemies and humiliated, to the experience of being rescued, forgiven, guided, loved and reassured. The Psalms are proof that Israel's God was absolutely approachable. The people can voice to God their praise and thanksgiving, their guilt and distress, their dismay over God's silence or apparent powerlessness, their impatience and outrage, their soul-searching and their desires, their wonder and their love. These prayers disclose the way the people of Israel experienced God. And Jesus knew those prayers, many of them probably by heart.

4. The Remembrance of the Prophets

Finally, there is *prophecy*. One could not have been living at the time of Jesus without ever having heard of the prophets. It was the prophets who read and discerned the signs of the times, and interpreted the nation's historical experience in terms of "the word of the Lord." However disturbing and unwelcome they may have been in their own times, the prophetic voices reassured the people that God had not given up on them. The people mattered enough to God that he sent them messengers to warn and correct them when they proved unfaithful, and to remind them of their responsibilities as God's chosen race. The remembrance of the prophets would have confirmed Israel's sense of election, because the existence of the prophets verified the historical presence of the Spirit of God among them. Whenever the prophetic voices grew silent, then Israel had reason to fear divine abandonment. The Christian community might draw the same point with respect to the appearance of saints throughout its history.

It is impossible to summarize in just a few lines what the various prophetic movements were all about, the historical circumstances surrounding each of them, and the content of the prophetic words. For that, one would best consult *The New Jerome Biblical Commentary* or the Reading Guide in *The Catholic Study Bible* (New York: Oxford University Press, 1990). Yet one thing that stands out clearly in the prophetic books is God's keen sensitivity about justice. Speaking through the prophets, God expresses intense outrage over the victimization of the poor and defenseless of the land. Justice appears to epitomize the meaning of the Law; infidelity to God can thus be summed

up as injustice. Jesus would certainly have been exposed to such prophetic sentiments as we find in Amos 8, or Micah 2, or the opening
verses of Isaiah 10:

> Woe to those who enact unjust statutes
>   and who write oppressive decrees,
> Depriving the needy of judgment
>   and robbing my people's poor of their rights,
> Making widows their plunder,
>   and orphans their prey! (Isa 10:1–2)

A second thing which draws our attention is the prophetic cri-
tiques of the political order. The prophets had a great deal to say about
what was wrong with the nation, about political events and national
destinies, and about the reshaping of history. This is an important point
to bear in mind. John the Baptist was the prophet whose message Jesus
heard, and before his career was finished, Jesus would be considered a
prophet as well. The prophets were famous for having meddled in the
nation's political and social affairs. Yet the appearance of a prophet
demonstrated that God was keeping the divine promise; the God who
sends Israel prophets is a God who is faithful. To remember the prophets, therefore, is to experience anew the historical dependability of
God. In fact, the appearance of Jesus would itself be the surest sign of
divine faithfulness.

The ideas we have just sketched deserve to be studied over an
entire semester, not in the meager space of a few pages. At least this
briefest of introductions provides a few basic ingredients of Jesus' religious world which would be more or less presupposed by the gospel
story. These ideas may help to sensitize the reader to the faith of Jesus,
which was also the faith of Israel, that lies beneath the surface of the
gospel narratives.

A Preliminary View of Jesus

Who was Jesus? First and foremost, he knew himself to be a
creature, made in the divine image and likeness, and dependent upon
the Spirit of God for every breath he drew. He was a person of uncom-
plicated faith who trusted that the God of Israel would never abandon

the people he had chosen and had delivered from slavery and exile. Jesus was someone who shared the spirit of Israel's experience before God and who knew God to be unbelievably close; he was a person for whom prayer was as natural an activity as breathing and eating. In prayer, the human heart was totally open to the sight of God; it was the one place where one never need be afraid to speak what was on one's mind, the place where one could stand in all honesty and humility, without the least fear of being rejected. And finally, Jesus stood in the tradition of the prophets, those mighty souls of the past who shared God's own feeling for the world and for Israel. Jesus knew how the Spirit of God had anointed the prophets so that they became witnesses to justice and proclaimed the word of God boldly and without fear. Sometimes in the nation's darkest hours, the prophets had helped keep alive Israel's confidence in the divine promise. The remembrance of the prophets would have played a critical role in Jesus' growing awareness of himself and his mission.

3

The Vision of "The Beginning"

Some years ago, a pastor in eastern Tennessee recounted something which had happened at the Easter Vigil service. The church was in darkness, save for a small light in the pulpit for the lector, who happened to be the mother of several small children. She began reading the opening words of the Book of Genesis, "In the beginning," in a manner that made them sound like "Once upon a time." Her voice captivated the congregation, who heard the great creation myth in a way they had never heard it before, warmly and with the feeling of a child's wonder. The pastor was thrilled. The biblical text had finally come alive as story.

Stories such as the opening chapters of Genesis are not *merely* stories. They create the world of meaning and symbol out of which we live and think, and define our place in the universe. True, they cannot be taken literally. There never were historical people named Adam and Eve, there never was a garden, it took more than "six days" to create the heavens and the earth, and the incident with the serpent leaves plenty of unanswered questions (such as, where the serpent came from and how it learned to speak). But the mind quickly concedes that such imaginative details simply pertain to the way people told stories at that time, and that the stories were never intended to be primitive metaphysical treatises. Thus, we can picture God strolling with Adam and Eve in the cool of the evening without being offended because the scene never actually took place. In the heart's desire, in the soul's great hope, this is the scene that we would like to see become real. Human beings long to be one with the Creator who lovingly brought them into existence, because union—being embraced totally and endlessly—is what we crave most.

Humanity's great hope, therefore, is embodied in a story about the past, in a myth about the origins of the human race. In that primeval garden, human beings walked comfortably with God, sharing thoughts and feelings, their souls totally open to the eye of God. They even walked naked before God and were unashamed. Not only that, but human beings were at peace and in communion with one another. God had made them male and female, fashioned according to the divine likeness, and radically equal. The freedom they enjoyed with God carried over into the way they related to one another. Communion and equality between human beings were possible because fear had not yet entered the story; there were no attempts to dominate or manipulate one another. And finally, human beings were one with the earth. The earth, and all that filled it, belonged to the Lord, who entrusted it to the care of his creatures.

But once sin entered the world, communion broke apart. Human beings became afraid of God and tried to hide from the one who had formed their bodies and breathed life into them. They were no longer one with the Creator. The man began to dominate the woman; thus human beings were no longer equal, which meant that society would now become patriarchal. Human bodiliness was sensitized to pain, sweat and the agony of childbearing, which implied that human beings were no longer at one even with their own bodies. And the earth suddenly appeared hostile, bringing forth "thorns and thistles." The earth itself, therefore, was no longer a willing mother to human beings. Now they would have to wrest its bountiful resources through hard labor. Humanity had become alienated from the earth. All of this can be found in the third chapter of Genesis.

In the eleventh chapter of Genesis we are told about the tower of Babel. One can picture a child sitting in its mother's or father's lap and asking why people spoke different languages. To the twentieth-century mind, the multiplicity of languages testifies to the extraordinary richness of human culture; we prize diversity and the splendidly variegated perspectives upon the world arising from the many different languages and cultures. To that biblical child and its parents, however, the multiplicity of languages pointed to a further rupture in humanity's primeval unity. They would account for the plurality of tongues by recalling a legend about human arrogance: "Come, let us build ourselves a city and a tower with its top in the sky, and so make a name for ourselves; otherwise we shall be scattered all over the earth" (Gen 11:4). Apparently such ambition could ultimately prove destructive, which may be why the Lord said, "nothing will later stop them from doing whatever they presume to do" (Gen 11:6). Perhaps the point is that any unity among human beings which is not founded upon a prior union with the Creator is bound to wreak havoc upon the human race through presumption. No matter how sophisticated they become, creatures will never outgrow their dependence upon the Creator who brought them to life and sustains them.

The Vision of the Beginning and the Kingdom of God

Now, if we are right in locating the seed of humanity's longing for union with God and communion with one another in the opening story of the Bible, then it would only seem right that the kingdom of God which Jesus preached would recapture the main elements of that distant hope and project them toward the future. The kingdom of God would be marked by a closeness between human beings and God which could best be described in terms of their being God's daughters and sons. Yet if they are daughters and sons of God, then that would automatically make them sisters and brothers, all of them. According to this vision, no one would become another's master (Gen 3:16); no one would manipulate or intimidate another, because they would stand before one another without fear. National boundaries would no longer exercise any determinative role in relationships between human beings, nor would racial or ethnic lines. Men and women would be radically equal as children of God: neither rich nor poor, neither patron nor slave. The kingdom of God, in other words, builds upon the most profound human hope. To announce the kingdom would be to stir that hope and appeal to an ancient memory buried deep within the human subconscious about how things were "once upon a time." That memory, however, is actually a vision or a dream; the Spirit of God can make it real.

PART TWO:
READING THE
GOSPEL STORY

4

Everything Starts with Easter Faith

Of the four gospels, perhaps the best place to start talking about Jesus is the gospel of Mark. Scholars tell us that Mark most likely wrote in the 60's, to a community of Christians living in Rome who faced the imminent threat of persecution. The gospel text has to be read slowly and carefully, and not once or twice, but six, seven or eight times, or until one is fully attending to the gospel as a story about the faith of Jesus, his followers, and the later community to which Mark belonged. Mark has shaped the gospel material to fit the needs, questions, concerns and experience of the community for which he was writing. Jesus' journey to the cross is a major motif; discipleship thus becomes a matter of being with Jesus on the way to Jerusalem and the cross. The way of discipleship entails a great deal of persecution, but this suffering is always in the context of companionship with Jesus.

The important thing to recognize at the outset, however, is that the entire composition of the gospel, from the first stroke of the evangelist's pen, is marked by Easter faith. Not only was Mark aware of the story's outcome, but also for the evangelist himself, as well as for the community around him (since he was not living and writing in scholarly seclusion) Jesus was a living presence, and the Christian community was an ark of salvation. The same would have been true for each of the gospel writers. For each of them, and for their communities, Jesus was alive and active among them. He was still gathering them, teaching them, reconciling them to one another, healing and loving them, and empowering them to continue his mission. Moreover, the gospel story was not written for the sake of the first disciples themselves, but for the sake of those who would be coming later, although none of the evangelists could have envisioned that their texts would have been reaching the ears of congregations some twenty centuries later. Had they done so, then the gospels would not have been shaped by the specific circumstances of the communities the evangelists knew, but by far more general concerns: so general, in fact, as probably to render their writing dull and useless. To write for every conceivable audience is to write for no one.

The Way We Live Conditions the Way We Approach the Gospels

Just as resurrection faith guided the composition of the gospel from the very first verse, and just as the abiding presence of Jesus was the presupposition which marked the evangelist's thinking, remembering and imagining as he shaped the stories and sayings of Jesus, as well as the memories about him; so also resurrection faith governs how we hear and study the gospels today. Whether we are aware of it or not, the risen Jesus has come alongside of us to open our eyes to the meaning of his story; this is an essential part of Christian experience (see Lk 24:13–35). However, if our living has not been colored by Easter faith, if the way we are currently living and acting would not be affected one way or the other by whether or not Jesus was raised from the dead, then that would mean we have yet really to hear the story of Jesus. Someone may have *told* us the story, but we would not yet have *heard* it.

The news about Jesus' being raised from the dead was not merely a consoling piece of information (actually, it was more puzzling, even startling, than consoling); rather, it was above all life-transforming news. It was a revelation about the real order of things, the inner secret or mystery of creation itself. Death, and all that death represented or symbolized, could never be viewed the same way again. The impact of this revelation was the setting free of human beings. Finally, they had been delivered from the power of death, which meant that at last they were free to live as children of God, delivered from the fear that would destroy their spontaneity, their integrity and their trust in God. The resurrection makes a difference as to the kind of human beings we choose to be.

Curiously enough, while Mark knew that Jesus had risen from the dead, and while Mark's readers would have known this, too, even before they began reading the gospel (since they were already Christians), and while we also know the outcome (since we, like Mark and his audience, are already familiar with the story of Jesus), Jesus himself and his disciples did not know what was going to happen, except in terms of their broad conviction that God's saving action in history cannot ultimately be frustrated. The failure to appreciate this merely confirms the mistaken impression which many have shared over the centuries that Jesus was only pretending to be human. If Jesus were already informed and assured of the outcome of his own story, then he was not like us. If he had known about a resurrection "on the third day" from the outset, then his story would have been robbed of the essential elements of faith and hope. But this is not something we are going to comprehend at the very beginning. It is seldom easy at the outset to allow Jesus to be fully human, since all of us tend to approach the story with a number of preconceptions as to what being the Son of God was all about.

5

The Reality of God

"This is the time of fulfillment. The kingdom of God is at hand. Repent, and believe in the gospel" (Mk 1:15).

For many of us, God could conveniently be removed from our mental world and our lives would probably not be markedly different. We would continue our routines, stay with our plans, work, study, and so forth, with only occasional and minimal conceptual adjustments. The reason for this may be that the benevolent God whom many people believe in does not really exist; *that* God is actually a dispensable consolation which is not truly needed for the proper functioning of the world and society, an expendable symbol of cosmic order and a transcendental (though hollow) guarantee of the rightness of things. And, curiously, the same may be true for many marginalized, poor people. God is not relevant to their lives, either. They would never deny the existence of God, but they would probably add that God has not been an essential part of their lives because the God about whom they have been taught belongs to the rich, the powerful, and those who have found places of security and respect in human society. But what has God done lately for the poor? Their lives, like those of the rich, would remain unchanged, whether God existed or not.

This observation occurred to me because of the striking contrast I have experienced between the world of the college where I teach, on the one hand, and life in the downtown neighborhood where I live, on the other. For whom, I ask myself, has God been more "real" or present? The college, set off on a hill overlooking the city, appears so immune to the world beneath it. Its concerns are educational and academic, even, one sometimes suspects, its attention to God. People send their children to a Jesuit college, a professor once half-jokingly remarked, to learn the secret of being able to serve both God and money, figuring that if any group had found its way around that gospel text, surely the Jesuits have! From the luxury of academic isolation, one thinks and talks about God in untested ways; if God did not exist, the world of higher education would still flourish. The people living below, however, make their way in a very different world. Food stamps, unemployment, teenage pregnancy, drugs, a smattering of prostitution and the ever-present threat of AIDS: such things provide faith with a very different sort of test. The number of churches in the neighborhood, some Catholic, others evangelical, attests to the fact that many people there still actually accept the existence of God; yet from the way they speak, God appears to be real to them in a largely unreal way. That is, God is the invisible friend or companion whose existence has little bearing upon the realities of everyday life.

For Jesus, God was eminently real. God did make a difference to the way he lived and thought. The gospel verse of Mark 1:15 resounds with conviction about the reality and nearness of God. "This is the time!" and "The kingdom of God is at hand!" announce that something new and different was about to begin. Yet, before God could again become real to human beings, their hearts had to change. The reason why God is not fully real to us lies not with God; the reason—indeed, the fault—generally lies with us and our absorption with ourselves. The poor may be excused from taking God seriously because they have not been presented with a credible picture of God by those who have professed to know God. Yet if God has not been real for us, either, then we have nothing to plead in our defense. Many of us would stand guilty of denying in practice, by the way that we think and act, that we are in fact creatures and that we owe fundamental obedience to the God of justice, who made us sisters and brothers to one another. To repent means above all to take God with the utmost seriousness; but how to do that? What does it mean to take God seriously? Perhaps the God we have grown to believe in has not yet become for us the God of Jesus, which would account for the major difference between us and him. The God of Jesus is the one to whom the gospel (and thus the Spirit of Jesus) is going to introduce us.

Let us consider the question, then, about how God is going to become real for us. Is it that God has been present among us, but we lack the right words to name that presence? Or is it that we might be lacking the very experience of God? Is it a fault of preaching and catechesis? Has the preached word been deficient in zeal and faith, so that people have not been inspired to seek and find God? Or have we been deprived of that authentic Christian witness which signals transcendence and causes us, stunned by heroic love, to raise our minds toward God? What exactly is the problem?

Not Just Any God, but the God of Jesus

The basic issue is not how to render God real, but rather how *the God of Jesus* becomes real. There are, after all, other avenues to the holy mystery of God besides being-with-Jesus. Taking our cue from the gospel story, I would suggest that the God of Jesus (who is the God of Israel) becomes real at the very point when we start to share what was of concern to Jesus, namely, the kingdom of God. And nothing brings us so close to that concern as being with those who are poor, who are hungry, who thirst for justice, who are powerless. Their experience of life and of the world becomes a privileged place for discovering the reality that we seek. The fact that the poor have often failed to discover the presence of God in their midst serves to underline why Jesus is so crucial to our understanding of God. The God about whom they have been told has frequently been the God of those on top, the God "from above" who dwells in splendor. Jesus' life radically challenges that misapprehension about what God is truly like. If we find ourselves lamenting the loss of our sense of the transcendent, or if our self-examination confirms the fact that God has honestly not been real to us, then our sole recourse is to look to the story of Jesus. The kingdom of God arises among those who desperately want and need it, who would welcome the saving, liberating presence of God's Spirit because they have been shut out from the good things of this world. The God whom Jesus knows is a God who is revealed "from below"; this God appears from within the world of those living at the bottom or on the margins of society. God becomes real, in other words, as we view the world through an entirely different lens. That lens is Jesus. Being-with-Jesus, one is introduced to a very different world and a very different reality. One soon begins to find oneself in another sort of company, so different, in fact, that those "on the outside" appear flat and dull, and completely out of touch with what ultimately matters in life.

6

Jesus' Conversion

There are three interconnected scenes in the opening chapter of Mark: (1) the preaching of John the Baptist, (2) Jesus' baptism by John in the Jordan and (3) Jesus' temptation in the wilderness. Jesus, presumably, would have heard about John, even in the remote hilltown of Nazareth. We are not told why he approached John at that particular time, but whether out of curiosity or for some other unknown reason, Jesus arrived with the crowds who had come to see and to hear the great prophet. In accepting John's baptism, Jesus declared his solidarity with all the people of Israel who wanted to change their hearts, or to repent, which was what John had been calling for. Jesus was one with them in their hope that once again God would prove faithful to the divine promise to liberate the people from oppression and install the reign of justice, righteousness and truth. In order to grasp what John the Baptist stood for, we would need to look at the gospels of Matthew and Luke which spell out the content of John's preaching, at least in the minds of these evangelists (Lk 3:3–18, Mt 3:7–12).

But John is also a prophet (a designation which later would be applied to Jesus, too). To shed light on John, and to shed light on why the people eventually identified Jesus as a prophet (indeed, *the* Prophet, according to the fourth gospel), one needs to review Israel's prophetic literature. One needs to recall the message and the history of figures such as Isaiah, Jeremiah, Ezekiel, Amos, Hosea and Elijah. John at the Jordan stands in continuity with their message, their voice and their fate. By accepting John's baptism, Jesus may even have been accepting the prophetic mantle, just as Elisha received it from Elijah, likewise at the river Jordan (2 Kgs 2:9–14). In fact, later Jesus will make a veiled reference to John as Elijah (Mk 9:11–13). Mark wants to stress Jesus' uniqueness, however, and thus he records that Jesus heard God's own voice addressing him as "my son, the one whom I love." Again, what exactly this could have meant for Jesus is not revealed to us. It would be a mistake to read into these words of address all the weight of later theological reflection about the identity of Jesus. Sonship, at this stage, bears a biblical, not a metaphysical meaning; a son of God is one who serves God with complete filial devotion, trust and love. For Jesus, the only thing which seems clear is that the moment of his baptism was indeed a profound religious encounter with the God of Israel. Jesus had turned toward God in accepting John's baptism, and God had now turned toward him, personally and intimately, for Jesus had just experienced God to be his Father.

Retreat to the Wilderness

The moment required time to be digested, and thus Jesus is driven into the desert, we are told, where he would be tempted. Tempted to what? Tempted to disbelieve or to distrust his experience? Tempted proleptically, as if facing in a symbolic, anticipatory way the sort of things God's messiah or deliverer might be expected to have to face? The image of the desert is already rich, suggesting, as it does, the place where the human spirit, alone and undistracted, confronts its own dark side and is purified in order to meet God face-to-face. Until this point, Jesus had led a remarkably uneventful life in Nazareth. In his recent study about the historical Jesus, John Meier states: "all signs point to an uneventful adolescence and adulthood spent at woodworking in Nazareth. However galling the gospels' silence about Jesus' 'hidden years' may be, the silence may have a simple explanation: nothing much happened. . . . Jesus in Nazareth was insufferably ordinary" (A Marginal Jew: Rethinking the Historical Jesus, pp. 351–52). It is no wonder, therefore, that upon experiencing God in so dramatic and unexpected a fashion he would be driven into the wilderness. Jesus would have needed time to understand his experience of God, which somehow was connected with the figure of John the Baptist and his message. God had suddenly pressed a claim on Jesus: the moment of his baptism was the moment of his being called.

However radical and decisive his conversion experience was, the fact that Jesus withdrew to the desert suggests that it did not automatically confer clarity with respect to his mission. Some contest or struggle had to occur. After all, one does not leave the familiar surroundings of hometown and family, find oneself stirred within the depths of one's soul as a result of an encounter with one of God's prophets, and then not have to come to terms with one's past, with one's family ties and with a future whose shape must have been fairly predictable, given Jesus' station and upbringing. Suddenly to find oneself face-to-face with a prophet, and to hear for oneself the prophetic insight into the political, religious and social situation of the times, and to be confronted with the critical belief that the time for God's decisive intervention in history is now, in one's very own day, is to be thrown into some sort of inner turmoil, the likes of which are only dimly intimated by the words, "At once the Spirit drove him out into the desert" (Mk 1:12).

Did Jesus Need to Repent?

But if John's baptism was a baptism of repentance, then it seems logical to ask, "Was Jesus a sinner?" Was he, like everyone else, acknowledging his need to repent and turn to God? The answer to this question is difficult to give, because the subsequent tradition came to believe that Jesus was sinless, and that he had to be sinless because otherwise he could not be a fitting high priest, nor could he be (to reverse the imagery) the unblemished sacrifice.

Jesus, we have to keep reminding ourselves, was fully human, and because he was human, he fit into the world like everyone else. He kept God's law, as he had been taught, and was, therefore, a righteous person. He was undoubtedly impatient and angry at times, reacting to people and events the way any normal human being would. Such demonstrations of feeling are neither sinful nor human imperfections. Jesus was not a Stoic. Some people construe various sorts of actions and reactions as sinful (particularly some of the stormy sexual feelings and fantasies of adolescence) which are simply normal human behavior. For a while, Jesus may even have hated the Romans. Hating one's enemy would not have constituted a sin, although a person growing in God would eventually move beyond this stage of feeling. Nor would being tempted constitute a sin: temptation and tension are part and parcel of the growth of the human spirit, too. In short, a person could theoretically live a normal human life, subject to all the moods, feelings, emotions and inner struggles that characterize the human condition, without ever committing a sin. One could understandably wonder whether it might even be possible to experience the sorry burden of the human condition without ever actually doing something morally wrong.

If we view repentance as the human being's turning radically and lovingly toward God, deciding as firmly and profoundly as the soul's liberty allows, to love God with all one's heart, soul, mind and strength; if we grant that every human being, simply because he or she is a creature, needs to express the reality of creaturehood by surrendering completely to God in an act of praise and worship; if one element of realizing that one is a creature is the awareness that one is always inadequate when standing face-to-face with the Creator, and that this inadequacy ordinarily comes to expression in the experience of being "sinful"; then it makes sense to say that Jesus, too, felt the need to repent. Jesus, like us, would have experienced the need and the desire to surrender completely to God. Jesus, like us, would have experienced the creature's inadequacy before the Creator, quite apart from the matter of ever having done anything contrary to God's law. Jesus could have stood before John the Baptist, honestly and humbly seeking to ritualize his turning toward God with all his heart, mind and soul, which was the substance of repentance.

Jesus' baptism, in other words, was not a mere formality, an edifying show of piety for the benefit of the crowds. For at the time, the people did not know him, nor would he have already attracted disciples: companions, perhaps, but not disciples. Later, other evangelists would touch up this scene in order to underscore the fact that Jesus was indeed superior to John (Jn 1:19–34), and that he did not actually need to be baptized (Mt 3:14). Clearly, the memory of Jesus' baptism was going to become something of a theological embarrassment in light of the church's developing faith: Why would the Son of God submit to such a thing? But the baptismal event was too important, too critical to the story, to be suppressed, in spite of later tensions which would erupt between the disciples of John and those of Jesus. Still, we must not allow those "corrective" tendencies to prevent us from hearing the basic fact that Jesus was indeed baptized by John. What might have been puzzling, even shocking to a later generation which had come to profess that Jesus was God's Son in an ever more exclusive way made perfect sense to Jesus himself. He came to be baptized by John because he was moved by John's message; he was baptized because he wanted to repent, to turn radically toward God, along with everyone else who went to the Jordan.

Although the evangelists do not mention this, it is not impossible that Jesus, moved by John's preaching, used the occasion to speak with him. Perhaps John prepared Jesus' way, not only by means of his preaching and his baptismal ministry at the Jordan, but also by assisting Jesus to discern the pathways of his own future. His sudden departure for the desert becomes more understandable if John the Baptist, a prophet thoroughly acquainted with the spirits and demons of the wilderness, had suggested that Jesus likewise retreat for a while to the desert in order to come to terms with the voice he had heard. Jesus' experience demanded that he follow the Baptist's lead.

7

Truth Confirmed by Experience

All were amazed and asked one another, "What is this? A new teaching with authority" (Mk 1:27).

How might we describe the figure of Jesus in the opening chapters of Mark? He is obviously being portrayed as a teacher, but where did he get his learning from? This question is natural enough to ask, considering that the villagers in Jesus' hometown would likewise raise this question a little later (see Mk 6:1–6). What sort of credentials did Jesus have? Obviously, he did not possess much of an academic background, which explains why his neighbors, the people around whom he had grown up, were utterly astonished. Moreover, Jesus does not teach in the manner of the scribes, those charged with studying, interpreting and teaching the law and the prophets of the Old Testament; rather, he teaches "with authority."

Yet what sort of authority is this, if Jesus lacks credentials, if he is not a lawyer or a priest, or if he has not been formally trained in reading and interpreting the scriptures? I think there are two reasons which might be offered. First, Jesus was charismatic; that is, he spoke and acted with a depth of conviction and a sincerity which moved other people to trust him. He said what he believed; he spoke from his experience and his faith. Secondly, Jesus had the authority which the people themselves conferred upon him. What Jesus did and said made perfect sense to them; he had affirmed their experience of life, too. Jesus spoke their language. His God was not distant, or legalistic, or the subject of learned disquisitions. The images which Jesus used in his teaching were drawn directly from the everyday world that even the humblest among them could relate to.

When the crowds noted that Jesus taught with authority, what they were in fact saying was that they trusted him. After all, there were other authorities around, namely, the professional religious leaders. Apparently, the crowds had not conferred the same sort of authority on them. The consequence of this would be a conflict of authority: Jesus, with the truth of his message, confirmed by experience, on the one hand; and the scribes, teachers of the law and the Pharisees assembled against him, on the other hand. Whatever differences would arise between the teaching of Jesus and the teaching of the others would become secondary. The basic issue would be one of authority, which the professionals soon twisted into one of power. They had just been challenged by a Galilean layman, and they did not like it.

After examining what can be distilled from the various sources available to us about the historical Jesus, John Meier drew a conclusion about the background of Jesus as teacher which is relevant here. He writes: "Jesus' teaching was delivered orally, and oral teaching could in theory have been the sole conduit of Jesus' own education in the scriptures and Jewish traditions. In the oral popular culture in which he grew up and later taught, literacy was not an absolute necessity for common people. Yet the matrix of a devout Jewish family, Jesus' own preoccupation with Jewish religion, and the debates over scripture that Jesus held with professional scribes and pious Pharisees during his ministry all make his ability to read the sacred text a likely hypothesis" (A *Marginal Jew*, pg. 351). This would confirm the point we have been making, namely, that the authority which the crowds conferred upon Jesus' teaching was not occasioned by academic or religious credentials, but by the message itself: its homegrown truth was confirmed by experience.

8

Signs and Wonders

"What mighty deeds are wrought by his hands!" (Mk 6:2)

One of the prominent features of the opening chapters of Mark is the miracles of Jesus. Not only did Jesus teach with authority; the gospel reports that he also acted with authority. The same conviction and faith which informed Jesus' words likewise appeared in what he did. His was not the behavior of someone absolutely confident that he possessed infallible curative powers; for the fact is that he did not. Rather, Jesus had the attitude of a person of faith who wholeheartedly trusted his experience of God. Jesus' working miracles is the closest we come to a gospel answer to the presence of evil in the world: God does not want it.

There are numerous healing episodes throughout the gospel narrative where Jesus, apparently seeking to avoid notoriety, asks the person cured to keep the miracle a secret. Perhaps these are instances of the evangelist wanting to alert his readers to the fact that there was more to being Son of God than working wonders. Yet, for the most part, in his first two chapters Mark seems to be presenting the miraculous healings as charismatic complements of Jesus' teaching. Actually, Mark never spells out the content of that teaching the way Matthew and Luke do. If Jesus teaches anything in Mark, maybe it is simply how to be with him as he makes his way to Jerusalem and the cross. What we are given are lessons in discipleship rather than learned discourses. The Jesus of Mark is a Jesus who journeys to the cross, and his disciples and companions are those who are willing to accompany him, in poverty and in freedom.

Some readers would view the miracles as confirmations of the truthfulness of Jesus' teaching; others would view them as confirmations of Jesus' authority and divinity. Nevertheless, the fact is that many people witnessed the miracles yet refused to accept Jesus' teaching, and the fact is, too, that other prophets worked miracles before Jesus. At the word of Moses, for example, the waters of the Red Sea were divided (Ex 14), and at the word of Elijah a dead child was restored to life (1 Kgs 17). No one concluded, however, that those figures possessed divine status or shared in the divine nature. Following the lead of liberation theology, I incline toward the view that the miracles are fundamentally signs of the kingdom and God's desire to liberate: not in the manner of glitzy pointers to the kingdom's imminent arrival, but as signs of the fact that God's will is truly to save human beings from all that oppresses them. God wants to liberate, not only from the oppressive political and economic forces that keep men and women poor, anxious and fearful, but also from physical infirmities, guilt and sin, even from the demonic assaults upon human freedom, integrity and decency which rob them of their sanity and their very humanity. The majority of Jesus' miracles can thus be read as protests against the evils which afflict human beings. God, the miracles are telling us, does not want to see men and women mentally, physically or spiritually tormented. In God's kingdom, suffering human beings will be liberated from every affliction.

Miracles as God's Protests against Human Suffering

Most readers generally have little difficulty accepting the miracles as part of the story about Jesus. Some, however, are naive literalists in the matter of miracles: they take them word for word as dramatic illustrations of Jesus' power. Others are suspicious. While they would not dare to excise the miracles from the gospel story, they remain content just to let them stand as one-time demonstrations of the truthfulness of the gospel. The miracles, they presume, authenticated Jesus' claims. Yet they are bothered by the fact that miracles are patently interruptions of the natural order of things, which raises disturbing questions about God. Why, for example, doesn't God heal *all* those who have various diseases? Why aren't miracles happening today? Why would God create a world where sickness and infirmity invade human life, only to turn around later and cancel them? Is God consistent, or does God have afterthoughts?

Unfortunately, the gospel does not answer speculative questions about God, the problem of evil in the world, or the meaning of suffering. Or maybe the lack of theological speculation by Jesus and the evangelists is meant to point our minds in a different direction. God is on the side of life and is absolutely good. Evil exists, and everyone, including Jesus, is painfully aware of its reality. But the fact of evil never erases Jesus' experience of God as both loving and concerned about men and women, who are, after all, God's children. If anything, the miracles represent divine protests against the misery and suffering which those children have to endure.

This approach to miracles still leaves the speculative questions unresolved, yet it does offer one definite advantage. By never compromising the conviction that divine saving action is always liberating (because God wills to set human beings free), one refuses to separate one's experience of the world from prayer. Prayer is the only place from within which one can begin to reconcile the apparent inconsistencies in his or her idea of God. As far as Jesus was concerned, suffering never presented itself as a speculative issue of theodicy which he had to unravel. The reason is not that Jesus was no philosopher, but that he found no inconsistency between his experience of God as his Father and the suffering and helplessness of men and women like himself.

In the episode of Jesus' being rejected by the people in Nazareth, Mark remarks that Jesus was unable to perform any miracle there because of their lack of faith, which "amazed" Jesus (6:5–6). That Jesus should be amazed reveals what a keen letdown he must have experienced. Coming home with good news about the imminence of God's kingdom, he meets derision and contempt instead of welcome. No wonder he disowned his own family! But what this scene also shows is that a miraculous event, detached from Jesus' vision of the kingdom, has no context. It would lack the proper interpretative horizon. That horizon, we have just noted, is nothing less than how God wants the world to be. Rather than viewing them as interrupting the natural order of things, one might do better to read the miracles as divine protests and as signs of God's desire to liberate: Jesus does not accept the world as it is, and neither does God. Now, perhaps, it becomes clear why Jesus kept demanding faith from people. A miracle is not a magical response on God's part to a person who prays, with eyes closed, "I do believe! I do believe!" Mountains are not going to rise up and cast themselves into the sea, fruit trees are not going to wither at someone's whim, and poisonous snakes are not suddenly going to lose their venom. There is nothing magical about God's action in history. Faith is not a suspension of belief, but a very conscious decision and disposition to allow the liberating reality of God into one's life, as Jesus did.

Another point about the miracles which deserves mention is that they were not staged in order to provoke the religious authorities; they ought not to be read this way, despite the fact that the miracles are often situated in confrontation episodes. Jesus offended the zealous Pharisees because they could not tolerate his healing on the sabbath. Apparently they had no problem with Jesus' working a miracle; it was the timing which irritated them. The conclusion they would have had to draw was either (1) that God did not care about the sabbath rest after all, which would have undermined the religious convictions upon which they had staked their lives, or (2) that Jesus' power to work miracles did not depend upon God, but upon the demons. It would be a mistake to think that the religious leaders would have knowingly placed themselves over and against God. Yet, in terms of Mark's story, that is exactly what they did, as soon as they made their problem with Jesus into an issue of power and authority instead of truth. The divine mystery hides itself from men and women who resort to power and fear instead of risking an encounter with truth and freedom.

The Effect of the Miracles: Restoration of One's Social and Economic Well-being

One vignette in the first chapter of Mark which catches my attention is the curing of Peter's mother-in-law, who was in bed with a fever. "He approached, grasped her hand, and helped her up. Then the fever left her and she waited on them" (Mk 1:31). One wonders, not so much how this episode found its way into the gospel story, but why Mark mentions the fact that Peter's mother-in-law "waited on them" once she was made well. Were Jesus and his friends hungry? Had the meal been delayed because Peter's wife was tending to her mother? Was she healed in order to expedite things at mealtime, or was her waiting on them simply an expression of gratitude on her part?

The fact is that the mother-in-law could have felt fairly useless at a time when her help was sorely needed. From the time of the fever's onset, she had probably not been of much use around the home, and it could well have been that she was an elderly woman besides. Her waiting on them, therefore, suggests that she had once again become an important part of the family, pitching into the domestic chores and carrying her weight. Her dignity and self-esteem had been rescued. As in so many cases, the effect of Jesus' miracle was the person's re-entry into normal social life. The leper presumably returned to his village (1:43–45), just as the paralytic was able to resume a normal life with his family (2:11), as did the demon-possessed Gerasene man (5:19), and the blind man of Bethsaida (8:26).

Yet the re-entrance into regular social life was frequently accompanied by a re-insertion into a village's economic life as well. To anticipate a reflection we shall be making shortly, it is important to note the very obvious point that a paralyzed person, for example, cannot work. If the person had been married and had a family to raise, and then suffered a tragic accident, then both he and his family would have become enormously dependent upon their relatives and neighbors; they might very well have been forced to survive at the brink of poverty and hunger. No wonder, then, that the paralytic of Mark 2 had been so laboriously carried to Jesus by four friends; they would surely have known the man's desperate state. They thus approached Jesus, not just because Jesus worked miracles, but because he worked miracles primarily to the advantage of the poor and the oppressed.

The very same thing would have been true of Bartimaeus, the blind beggar who accosted Jesus on the Jericho road (Mk 10:46–52). Because he was blind, Bartimaeus had been reduced to a life of begging. At one point Mark reports, "Whatever villages or towns or countryside he entered, they laid the sick in the marketplaces and begged him that they might touch only the tassel on his cloak; and as many as touched it were healed" (6:56). This is an extraordinary scene. Ordinarily, the first (and only) thing to strike the reader's eye is the wonderful power Jesus had; we fail to meditate on the import of Jesus' action, or the setting. The marketplace would have been the site of commerce, where produce was brought from the countryside, where women went out each morning to procure grain and vegetables, oil and fruit, perhaps some meat or some fish from the lake. The presence of the sick and infirm in the marketplace lies in stark contrast with the good things for sale in the shops and stalls, for those who had money to buy them.

In the healing accounts, people regained their physical wholeness, yet there is another side to their being cured. They are restored to independence and once more have the possibility of finding employment and work, thereby participating again in the social life of their village or town, and the domestic life of their families. This aspect of the miracles of Jesus should never be overlooked; the people who were bringing their sick to Jesus would have known very well what the economic consequences of such infirmities were. Apart from this realization, Jesus becomes little more than a faith-healer, carrying on his healing ministry more or less oblivious to the political, social and economic realities around him. Only rarely do the well-to-do, maybe a person like Jairus, the synagogue official (Mk 5:22), or the Roman centurion concerned for the life of his slave (Lk 7:2) request a miracle (although even in these cases, the requests are coming from people whose faith has made them aware of their real condition before God). Jesus' healing activity seems to take place largely among the economically vulnerable and socially marginalized people of the land. This itself reveals a great deal about the message which must have accompanied his miracles.

Restoration to social and economic wholeness is another important aspect of God's desire to liberate human beings from all that oppresses them. The miracles reveal a major facet of Jesus' sensitivity to men and women in distress. His signs and wonders are for the poor, reversing, as they do, at least one of the conditions which keep them impoverished.

Let me add a brief postscript. While narrating some accounts of Jesus' healing activity, Matthew's gospel at one point includes a curious quotation from Isaiah 53, a text we normally associate with the passion story:

> "He took away our infirmities
> and bore our diseases." (Mt 8:17; cf. Isa 53:4)

Daniel Harrington notes that by citing this "fulfillment text" in connection with Jesus' miracles, Matthew has pulled Jesus' healing activity into the mystery of his suffering and death (*The Gospel of Matthew* [Collegeville: The Liturgical Press, 1991], p. 117). This insight radicalizes the idea of miracles as protests still further, for the suffering and death of Jesus is itself a direct consequence of the evil and alienation which exists in the world and from which all of creation is groaning to be set free (see Rom 8:21–22). The whole of Jesus' life, which culminates in his execution and resurrection, might thus be viewed as both a cry for justice or a protest against the world as it is, and a prayerful cry for the kingdom of God to come quickly.

9

The Call Stories

As he passed by, he saw Levi, son of Alphaeus, sitting at the customs post. He said to him, "Follow me." And he got up and followed him (Mk 2:14).

In their effort to heighten dramatic effect, storytellers often abbreviate things. Countless readers of the gospels have been edified, even inspired, by the response of the disciples to Jesus. In the opening chapter of the gospel, Mark narrates the calling of the first disciples. They were at work, fishing, as Jesus passed by. He paused, watched, and then invited them to follow him. Immediately, we are told, they put down their nets and joined him. In each of the gospel accounts, the call stories bring out the quickness of the disciples' response to Jesus' words, "Follow me." One could ponder those scenes at length, trying to recapture imaginatively the sentiments and dispositions of those men who went after Jesus so readily and, apparently, so completely. In laying aside their nets, for example, they were in fact saying farewell to their past: to their livelihood, to everything they had come to depend upon for security, to the familiar world of the lake where, as fishermen, they had been in control. Mark mentions that James and John even left their father Zebedee "in the boat along with the hired men" (1:20). The moment illustrates the radical nature of discipleship, leaving even one's family and friends for the sake of the gospel. Much later, Peter would remind Jesus, "We have given up everything and followed you" (10:28). And driving home the point that these followers had truly renounced every security in order to be with Jesus, the fourth gospel recalls a low moment when a large number of disciples, distressed by something Jesus had said, decided to return to their former way of life. Jesus asked the Twelve, "Do you also want to leave?" To which Peter replied, "Master, to whom shall we go?" (Jn 6:66–68)

Actually, the episode from John restores a little naturalness to the call stories, at least in a negative way, by telling us that not all of Jesus' followers remained steadfast. At some point in their lives, Jesus proved to be too much for a number of them. Yet the overriding impression one forms from the call stories is that the disciples reacted to Jesus' invitation in an exemplary manner which the rest of us should aspire to imitate: their response was immediate, complete, and with no regretful looking back. Luke records Jesus saying, "No one who sets a hand to the plow and looks to what was left behind is fit for the kingdom of God" (Lk 9:62).

One wonders, however, whether it was realistic to expect that everyone whom Jesus encountered would respond so quickly and positively. If so, then the gospel text might leave some of us feeling a little second-class, even a bit guilty. Many people are not at all sure that they would have responded to Jesus the way Peter and his companions did. What Mark's version of the call stories does is to exaggerate the ascetical features of being called and to underline the specialness of Jesus. From the vantage of resurrection faith, of course, such a response makes consummate sense. Who would not respond to the Jesus now known to be the Son of God in such a generous, surrendering way? At the time, however, the disciples did not know who Jesus was or what he stood for. One would conclude, therefore, that Mark is retelling the call story from the Easter side of the disciples' experience; this is the only way it makes sense.

I can recall visiting Rhode Island's Narragansett harbor one Sunday afternoon in late winter. There, on one of the piers, four fishermen were repairing enormous, steel-mesh nets. Their boat was docked alongside. "Son of a bitch!" one of them shouted. The wind was bitterly cold, which must have made the nets feel like blades of ice. Another one exclaimed, "This fucking net sucks!" The others roared with laughter. The Jesuit who had accompanied me turned to me and said, "Imagine coming to the likes of them and saying, 'How would you like to drop everything here and come help me start a church?' " We both began laughing, but his observation struck me as fairly close to the mark. One would have had to be absolutely naive to think that men such as these would suddenly lay everything aside and devote themselves thereafter to the things of God.

As a matter of fact, we know that Peter had a family, since shortly after meeting Jesus, we find him bringing Jesus to his home, where he cures Peter's mother-in-law. And it is quite probable that Peter invited Jesus to share his home in Capernaum, which, for a while anyway, served more or less as the center of his ministry. That was where people ordinarily came to meet or to listen to Jesus. And after the death of Jesus, John would have us believe that some of the disciples, at least temporarily, resumed their former occupation and went back to fishing (Jn 21). In all likelihood, the disciples continued to work even after Jesus had called them. They, and their families, would still need to survive. Jesus had not exempted them from their responsibilities and commitments to their wives and children. In fact, it would not be unreasonable to think that, while residing in Capernaum, Jesus would have found employment, too, so as not to be a burden on Peter's family. After all, Jesus did have a trade. A great deal of his teaching appears to have taken place in synagogues, on the sabbath, when people were free. The other days, perhaps, Jesus worked like the others, which could have meant that people gathered to converse with Jesus, and to hear him, and to bring him their sick relatives and friends, in the evening.

The Call Stories Had to Have Their Histories

It makes better sense to propose that the histories behind the gospel accounts of the calling of the disciples have been considerably abbreviated. Could we not imagine that Peter and Andrew, James and John, and the others, would have had a history to their contact with Jesus? Could it not be that they, too, had met him, perhaps been aroused by his words, attracted by his personality? The one who was going to draw men like Peter (if that scene on the Narragansett pier is any guide) could certainly not have been a wimp. He had to be like them in many ways, not the least of which would have been his experience of hard work, of struggling to survive, just as they did. He could not have been unfamiliar with the tensions, the problems, as well as the joys, of family life. He would have shared their resentment at having to pay taxes to support an occupying army, not to mention their frustration at not finding work, or their sense of being powerless to bring about change in their lives and in their land. No, the response of the disciples to Jesus has to have had a history (or, to state the same thing in different terms, their formal discipleship as "the Twelve" had its pre-history). They would have had to meet him, hear him, observe him. No one was going to make an immediate and complete surrender to a stranger, even to a stranger with the reputation of being a prophet or miracle-worker (a reputation which, at that point of the story, Jesus had not yet earned). They would have needed time to become acquainted with one another, to share stories about their past, their hopes, their opinion of John the Baptist and the meaning of the Baptist's message, their exasperation over the way things were going in the land, and so forth.

The same thing could be said of the call of Levi, the wretched tax-collector. Given the miserable reputation of tax-collectors in the gospel tradition, the rest of the disciples could hardly be expected to have given him a hearty welcome. To be sure, Jesus had shown himself to be a friend of tax-collectors and prostitutes, but the disciples would probably not have considered themselves as actually belonging to that kind of company. It serves no purpose to suggest that Jesus selected Levi in order to add some diversity to his group, as if Levi would be the token tax-collector, just as Mary Magdalene would be the token prostitute. Jesus did not have everything figured out in advance according to some master plan, even to the deliberate inclusion of Judas so that the betrayal could later take place. Nothing was figured out ahead of time; there was no script, no preordained divine plan to be executed. The evangelists do not explain why Levi caught Jesus' attention. They merely let us know that Jesus came to his defense (and the defense of the other "sinners" who had joined them for dinner at Levi's house) by saying that healthy people do not need a doctor; only sick people do (Mk 2:17; Mt 9:12).

There is an outside chance that it was Jesus who came to Levi's attention, as the authors of *Un tal Jesus* suggest. After all, Levi was collecting the taxes, and Jesus was passing by the tax-collector's booth. Suppose Levi was the one who stopped Jesus, insisting that Jesus pay his toll; then what? Then we have some way of accounting for how they met one another. A simple, direct invitation to Levi leaves the imagination begging for help: why would Levi have given up his lucrative job at the bidding of a stranger? One would have to conjecture that either Jesus was already known to large numbers of people as the great prophet from Galilee, or that Levi is responding to Jesus as if he were in on the secret of Jesus' identity as the Messiah or God's Son. If Jesus was already known to many people, then we might try to unravel Levi's mental state as a man suffering from implacable guilt, waiting day-by-day at the tax-collector's table for God in his mercy to deliver him from his sinfulness. Then, one day, Jesus arrives on the scene, sees him (and apparently sees into him), and Levi's life is changed. Whatever the circumstances of their initial encounter, personally, I would incline toward the view that, as in the case of the others, there was a history to the relationship between Jesus and Levi. There may be a sudden conversion experience implied by the story, but normally such dramatic turnarounds have some pre-history.

Some sort of imaginative reconstruction of the call stories needs to take place, therefore, if the stories are not to appear so miraculous that ordinary mortals like us feel left out and incapable of the same sort of heroic response as the first disciples. Besides, the narrative which ensues scarcely presents a flattering portrait of the disciples. Their subsequent behavior shows them to be all too human, constantly misunderstanding Jesus, quarrelsome, competitive, timid, boastful, and so on. Yet they stay with Jesus, right up until their fearful flight on the night Jesus was betrayed. If Jesus had not taken the initiative after his resurrection of reassuring the disciples of his love, rebuilding their self-confidence and their faith, and rescuing their hope, then their memory of Jesus for the rest of their lives would have been tinged with remorse and guilt.

The disciples did not leave everything and follow Jesus, literally, right at the beginning. Humanly speaking, that would not have been impossible, but it certainly would have been unrealistic or irresponsible, particularly if any of them were trying to provide for families. The fact is that they did not become his companions, in the beginning, because they believed him to be the Son of God. Other things had to happen first, chief of which would have been the resurrection itself, before they could understand what being Son of God was all about. Our realization that the call stories have to have had their histories makes it possible for us to relate to the gospels more personally, for what is reported to have happened in the story of Jesus and his disciples happened to real human beings, who were basically not much different from us.

10

Confrontations

They sent some Pharisees and Herodians to him to ensnare him in his speech (Mk 12:13).

Sometimes the radicalness of the gospel story is concealed by the rather conventional way many of us live out our faith. Yet the way Jesus must have come across to many people of his day was anything but conventional, and this raises for us the question as to what kind of disciple we want to be: conventional, or radical and counter-cultural? That will depend upon how seriously (and, in some cases, how literally) we choose to take the gospel. It is exhilarating to hear a gospel reader cry out in exasperation, "Did Jesus really expect people to do this? Are we supposed to take him literally?" Exclamations such as this are signs that readers are being engaged by the gospel story and that the original video within their imaginations is in the process of being replaced.

A number of scenes in the early chapters remember Jesus in various confrontations. First, there is the defiance of the demons: "In their synagogue was a man with an unclean spirit; he cried out, 'What have you to do with us Jesus of Nazareth? Have you come to destroy us?' " (Mk 1:23–24). Several verses later, Mark notes that "he drove out many demons" (1:34) and that he went "driving out demons throughout the whole of Galilee" (1:39). Next, there is the confrontation with religious authorities: "Now some of the scribes were sitting there asking themselves, 'Why does this man speak that way? He is blaspheming. Who but God alone can forgive sins?' " (2:6–7) This was clearly an issue over authority, because Jesus answers them, "But that you may know that the Son of Man has *authority* to forgive sins on earth . . ."

(2:10). And again, "Some scribes who were Pharisees saw that he was eating with sinners and tax collectors and said to his disciples, 'Why does he eat with tax collectors and sinners?' " (2:16) In the context, the question is not innocent; it bears an indirect reproach of Jesus' behavior. Jesus' choice of table fellowship left something to be desired. Or again: "At this the Pharisees said to him, 'Look, why are they doing what is unlawful on the sabbath?' " (2:24) By the time we arrive at the scene in the synagogue involving the man with a withered hand and another sabbath healing, the Pharisees are exasperated. They are prepared to conspire with the political arm (whose interests must also have been threatened by something Jesus had done or said) to bring about Jesus' death. Yet here we are, only a few verses into chapter three, still relatively early in the story! Mark writes, "The Pharisees went out and immediately took counsel with the Herodians against him to put him to death" (3:6).

The disciples of John the Baptist may also have figured into these confrontation episodes, at least if one can reasonably read between the lines. For we are told that the disciples of John the Baptist, like the Pharisees, were accustomed to fast (Mk 2:18). Some people took offense at Jesus' unascetical behavior, even to the point of labeling Jesus a glutton and a drunkard (Lk 7:34, Mt 11:19), which picked up an Old Testament reference to the "stubborn and unruly son" whose parents could have him executed for being "a glutton and a drunkard" (Deut 21:20), the prototype of the runaway boy in Luke's story of the lost son (Lk 15:11–32). Perhaps Jesus was similarly regarded by some back in his village as the stubborn and unruly son who had run away in order to eat and to drink, and to enjoy bad company. If so, that would help to account for the other group which Jesus had offended, and with whom he had a confrontation, namely, his own family:

> When his relatives heard of this they set out to seize him, for they said, "He is out of his mind." The scribes who had come from Jerusalem said, "He is possessed by Beelzebul" (Mk 3:21–22).

It appears that the family of Jesus and the scribes were in agreement, in much the same way that the Pharisees and the Herodians had joined forces earlier.

These various confrontations at the very beginning of his ministry serve to highlight for us the reality of Jesus' being a sign that would be contradicted (Lk 2:34). He disappointed as many expectations as he excited and fulfilled. This should help us to appreciate all the more the radical nature of Jesus' way. And unless Jesus had a heart of stone, this experience of resistance, suspicion, hostility, constant badgering, rejection by his own family and the people around whom he had grown up, not to mention his realization that others wanted to murder him (how does one reconcile oneself with this?), would certainly have played a part in his developing sense of what the kingdom of God was all about. It would surely, too, have entered into his growing awareness of what it meant to be the one with whom the Father was well pleased. One conclusion, at least, is inescapable. What happened to Jesus could also very likely happen to those who walked in his company and gradually shared in his experience of God. When Jesus later spoke to his companions about the risk of giving up everything for the sake of the gospel (Mk 10:29), he knew from experience what he was talking about.

11

The Lord of the Sabbath

I can remember attending Sunday mass as a youngster and listening to the gospel story about Jesus walking through the grainfields on
the sabbath day with his disciples, and wondering why the Pharisees
were trailing behind them. Years later, as the New Testament class I
was taking was winding its way through various gospel commentaries, I
recalled that early puzzlement and smiled. Indeed, we learned, the
Pharisees should not have been in the scene. The same commandment
which would have prohibited the work of picking grain on a sabbath
day also forbade a person's walking beyond a specified distance. If the
Pharisees had really been tracking Jesus and his companions, they
would also have been violating the sabbath rule, since a group walking
through the middle of a grain field was clearly in the countryside. As a
result, scholars have concluded that this episode, like a number of
others, is a Marcan construction. The evangelist was intending to
register a faith-claim about Jesus, namely, that Jesus was Lord of the
Sabbath. What the early community was maintaining, in effect, was
that Jesus was the authentic interpreter of the Law and the prophets,
the true scribe; even more, that Jesus was on a higher plane than the
Law and all it represented. Thus, he was not only the equal of Moses,
who had given the people of Israel the Law; he was even a greater
prophet and teacher than Moses, the liberator and lawgiver who had
spoken with God face-to-face.

A number of the early gospel scenes take place on sabbath days.
Behind each of them lies some christological claim. As the "Son of
man," Jesus has authority to forgive sins (Mk 2:10). He has authority
over demons and the counter-kingdom of Beelzebul (Mk 1:21–26). He
has the authority to interpret the true intention of the Law (Mk 3:4).

And because the sabbath was made for the sake of man, the Son of man has the authority to do on the sabbath whatever is for the welfare of human beings (Mk 2:27–28). In other words, in God's eyes the well-being of men and women counts much more than any human regulation or institution, no matter how venerable. Moreover, these christological claims are at the same time ecclesiological: whatever Jesus has the authority to do, the community of his disciples has the same authority to do. And the reason for this is not that Jesus has channeled to his community the authority which he first received from the Father. Rather, the reason is that no one controls the grace and Spirit of God; there are no official "channels." Jesus' attitude is radically communal; he envisions a community wherein all are brothers and sisters, and thus where all have equal access to the love and mercy of God. All members of the community, for example, have the power or the authority to assure one another of God's forgiveness. The conviction behind the question of the Pharisees that God alone can forgive sins (Mk 2:7) is right on target. Only God can forgive sins because only God can heal the human heart at its core, which is what the mystery of forgiveness is all about. The forgiveness which Jesus (and his community) brings, therefore, is always God's gift; men and women have the "authority" to assure their sisters and brothers that God's gift is really and truly given to them because God is really and truly their Father. What is at stake here, therefore, is the way God is. God is far more merciful, and closer, than most people had apparently realized. The coming of the kingdom brings with it the immediacy of God.

What Made Jesus' Teaching and Actions So Offensive?

Nothing in these episodes seems grave enough to warrant Jesus' death, and yet that is exactly what the Pharisees and Herodians began plotting (Mk 3:6). But what was so offensive or threatening about the fact that Jesus assured someone of God's forgiveness, or healed a paralytic, or restored a withered hand, or plucked grain on the sabbath? Certainly, as we have seen, according to Mark's version of the story Jesus had taken on the religious establishment; the issue between them had become one of authority. But lurking behind the scenes is God's true rival: not the Law or the faded religious institutions of Israel, but money. One suspects that wherever the religious leaders and the political powers have mutual interests, power, status and money have to be at stake. This is going to become clearer as the gospel story unfolds, although such collusion, together with the worship of money, never surfaces so openly that the true nature of Jesus' conflicts with authority appears in all its stark, ugly dimensions.

There is hardly any proportion between plucking grain on the sabbath and the determination to destroy Jesus. But what might render the hatred and suspicion of the authorities intelligible to us would be the fact that Jesus and his companions were making a path right through someone's field, and that they were picking the heads of grain because they were hungry. The motive for their behavior, therefore, was by no means to register a fancy christological claim about who the real Lord of the Sabbath was; the underlying motive was hunger. That is the force of Jesus' reference to the example of what David did *"when he was in need and he and his companions were hungry"* (Mk 2:25). Therefore, what Jesus as the Lord of the Sabbath had done was to tilt the Law and all it represented toward the benefit of the poor and those who were in need, even at the expense of the local landowners. The hidden issue in this scene was thus not about how much work one could legally engage in on the sabbath; it was about taking what belonged to someone else when human need required it. Now, if that is what was going on, the opposition to Jesus, which appears to have escalated fairly soon and fairly fast, becomes far more comprehensible.

The healing of the man with the withered hand drives the point home even further. First of all, it is quite clear that the man's infirmity had no connection with any wrongdoing; in other words, it was not a divine chastisement. As authentic interpreter of the religious traditions of Israel, Jesus in effect was reversing any thinking which would suggest that God inflicted physical suffering upon men and women as a punishment for sin. Secondly, it is also quite probable that a man with a withered hand would not be able to do much work, and not being able to work effectively could spell hunger, impoverishment and death. That is why Jesus asked whether or not it was lawful on the sabbath "to save life" (3:4). In itself, a withered hand would not be a life-threatening condition; but coupled with unemployment, it could spell economic and social disaster for the man and, presumably, his family. The reader might not immediately appreciate all of this, but the Pharisees and Herodians surely did. So did the rich. To be Lord of the Sabbath, in short, was to become the champion of those who were economically poor, legally defenseless and politically oppressed. It was also to be Lord of the Sabbatical Year: the year of freedom and liberation, the year of homecoming and the redistribution of property, which we read about in Leviticus 25. In brief, to be Lord of the Sabbath was to be the Lord of Justice. And this, we have to conclude, is precisely what Jesus was.

12

The True Family

But he said to them in reply, "Who are my mother and [my] brothers?" And looking around at those seated in the circle he said, "Here are my mother and my brothers. [For] whoever does the will of God is my brother and sister and mother" (Mk 3:34–35).

The third chapter of Mark contains an unsettling remembrance. Jesus has just returned "home" to Capernaum, presumably to Peter's household. Meanwhile, news of what had been happening had filtered back to Nazareth. "When his relatives heard of this they set out to seize him, for they said, 'He is out of his mind' " (3:21). These relatives must have included Jesus' mother and brothers, for they are the ones who arrive on the scene in verse 31. The news which they had heard about miraculous healings, confrontations with religious authorities, the gathering of followers, the forgiving of sins, and who knows what else, must have struck them as absolutely bizarre. So odd was Jesus' behavior that the scribes who had come from Jerusalem concluded that he had been possessed by a demon (3:22).

We have been so accustomed to believing that all things must have been well between Jesus and his family (since his would have been a model family), and so habituated into reading the "brothers" and "sisters" of Jesus as his "cousins," that the scandal and hurt suggested in this episode remain tucked away in the text. The first point to notice is that the family of Jesus believed that he had gone crazy. Having heard about what Jesus had been saying and doing since he left Nazareth, when he went to the Jordan in order to listen to John the Baptist, they set out to seize him. If persuasion failed, were they planning to overpower him and tie him in a straitjacket? Clearly, the Jesus about whom they were hearing was behaving very differently from the way they formerly knew him at Nazareth. Later we learn that the other townspeople, not only Jesus' relatives, were equally amazed at the change which had come over him: "Where did this man get all this? What kind of wisdom has been given him? What mighty deeds are wrought by his hands! Is he not the carpenter, the son of Mary, and the brother of James and Joses and Judas and Simon? Are not his sisters here with us?" (Mk 6:2–3) Jesus had not been famous for his oratorical skills or his insight into the scriptures, let alone for any power to work miracles. He was just the village carpenter, or the town handyman, known for being able to repair a fence or a door, or build a table, or fix a plow. If anything, the sudden change in Jesus indicates the ordinariness of his manner and the uneventfulness of his life up until the time of his being baptized and hearing the Father's voice.

Jesus Came from a Human Family

The second thing to notice is that, at least as far as Mark is concerned, Jesus belonged to a real family. He even seems to have had siblings. While this would hardly have been scandalous to his companions at the time, it is something which the Christian tradition subsequently blocked out in order to safeguard the virginity of Mary. Needless to say, this touches directly upon one of the most sensitive points of the Catholic tradition. It is also one of the most bothersome for many younger people today who want desperately to be, and to be considered as, intelligent, devout and loyal Catholic Christians, but who could never fully assent to the belief in Mary's virginity. If they choose to be intelligent and critical, they cease being loyal; yet neither can they remain simply one of the devout faithful, if that should require sacrificing their reason. Some are willing to grant that maybe God worked a miracle in Mary's conceiving Jesus, but they do not see either why this would have been necessary or what sort of signal God wanted to send to the human race about marriage and sexuality, which, after all, God had created.

Of course, God could still be Jesus' Father even if Jesus had a human father, because God could never be a biological parent of anyone. God was the Creator, and all human beings were already children of God in the most real sense: real enough so that Jesus could turn to those sitting around him and call them truly his sisters and brothers. For the way men and women prove that they are God's children is by listening to God in order to do what God wants. God's being Father of Jesus transcended genealogy, heredity and sexual passion. "Father" and "son" are relational terms: the meaning of the terms is ultimately evidenced in the way that the two relate to one another and interact. And this goes beyond the mere fact of being someone's biological father, as anyone knows whose actual fathering—whose nurturing and raising, whose being loved and cared for—was done by someone other than his or her biological parent.

Jesus: Single for the Sake of the Kingdom of God

It can be safely stated that Jesus was a celibate and single for the sake of the kingdom of God. However, he did not embrace celibacy out of some abstract ascetical ideal, but as one of the practical consequences of his radical turn toward God and his being called for mission. His choice (if he ever actually thought it through) had never meant a negative judgment about marriage, as if being single were intrinsically nobler or of a higher state than married life. The thinking of the Christian ascetical tradition eventually moved in that direction, but this would not have been Jesus' outlook. Being single was a practical consequence of his spirit's being seized for God's cause. While it is often mentioned that Jesus asked individuals to sell their possessions and give to the poor, it is never recorded that he asked someone to renounce marriage. Married people would have to learn how to leave everything for the sake of the gospel the same way single people would. It would be nearly impossible to imagine Jesus asking Peter, for example, to abandon his wife and family in order to become a missionary. And it would be next to impossible to imagine Jesus' God asking that, either.

The perpetual virginity of Mary should not to be allowed to become a stumbling block to faith. Perhaps the virginal conception functions as a symbolic device which affirms Jesus' unique relationship with God. That, of course, would involve us in the gospels of Matthew and Luke. But Mark, too, believed that Jesus was the Son of God, and as far as Mark was concerned, Jesus' being God's Son did not exempt him from being misunderstood even by those who were closest to him;

nor did it mean that Mary would be prevented from having other children after Jesus. Here one needs to consult some contemporary and careful Catholic biblical scholarship, such as Joseph Fitzmyer's helpful (and newly revised) book A *Christological Catechism*, or John Meier's study, which I have already cited (see chapter eight). Furthermore, Jürgen Moltmann's discussion of Jesus' "birth in the Spirit" approaches this issue, from the Protestant side, with great theological balance (*The Way of Jesus Christ*, pp. 78–87). At any rate, the tradition about the virginal conception ought not to distract us from paying full attention to Jesus. For many people today, this would have been an odd sign on God's part for underlining the uniqueness of Jesus; it would have exempted Jesus from the human condition in an area where we really need him to be like us. At best, the virginal conception could only be a sign. From a theological perspective, it would not confer something more on Jesus than the bestowal of the Spirit at his baptism, or the bestowal of new, definitive oneness with the Father at the supreme moment of the resurrection.

To repeat the point, Jesus' audience would not have taken offense over his having real sisters and brothers and not merely brothers in the broad sense of "cousins"; but a modern audience, raised on a different version of the story, might well be scandalized. What might very well have proven troublesome to some readers then and now, however, is the fact that Jesus disowned his family.

The Conclusion: Something Had Changed about Jesus

Once again, if one can read between the lines, it appears that, as Mark tells the story, people very close to Jesus simply failed to comprehend what had happened to him. Some of them eventually may have come to understand what he was saying and to share his enthusiasm for the promise of God. Jesus mightily believed that the divine promise was about to be fulfilled, although there were some things which Jesus himself could not have foreseen. Specifically, he would not have been able to foresee all that God was going to accomplish through him, for the future was not in Jesus' hands, but in the Father's. At any rate, Jesus' family and friends probably ought not to be blamed for their reaction to him. It is hard enough for any of us to accept prophetic voices into our lives, let alone prophetic relatives. Hence, Jesus' remark, "A prophet is not without honor except in his native place and among his own kin and in his own house" (Mk 6:4). How could Jesus have expected anything different from them? After all, it was he who had undergone the change, not they. And even if they had been disposed to believe in the gospel, their pride would have prevented them from acknowledging that someone so ordinary as the town carpenter could be the bearer of God's great promise to set people free.

Again, the dramatic change which had occurred in Jesus needs to be underlined. When he turned around and acknowledged those sitting around him as his real family, he was expressing the radical change of perspective that faith brings. What brings men and women close, what defines the way they relate to one another, is not bloodlines but the awesome truth that each of us comes from God. To live out that truth is to set oneself apart from the everyday world which is so treacherously familiar, because the everyday world often hides the truth from us. We can be living with people with whom we have very little left in common except blood ties, or merely verbal agreements to remain together. The everyday world can obscure the fact that relationships have become lazy and may have degenerated to the point of being lies. For Jesus, what defines the terms "brother," "sister," and "mother" is one's underlying relationship with God. Are we prepared to do God's will, or not? Are we prepared to let the things of God count above everything else in our lives, or not? The same sort of thinking governs Jesus' directive that we should address no one on earth as "father," since God alone could truly be father (and mother) to us (Mt 23:9). The experience behind such texts is revolutionary in that it overthrows the perspective of the everyday world and throws into relief the way God views things. Jesus had little choice but to disown his family. They were not thinking as God does, but as human beings do.

13

The One Who Speaks Out

One of the challenges in retelling the story of Jesus today comes from attempting to provide a sense of the social and political background of his life and times. There is a lack of clear, accessible material that describes the situation in which Jesus preached and which truly complements the gospel narratives. The liberation theologians have tried to do this, and I believe that they succeed, although some biblical scholars dispute the tendency of liberation theology to reduce so much of Jesus' activity into political, social and economic terms. The work of the Uruguayan Jesuit Juan Luis Segundo, *The Historical Jesus of the Synoptics*, for example, is one of several studies which manages to situate historically the conflict and tension which Jesus encountered. If Jesus was a prophet in continuity with the prophetic tradition of Israel, then he necessarily would be drawn into attacking the injustice suffered by his people. The kingdom of God was incompatible with every form of tyranny and oppression. This makes the death of Jesus far more intelligible than the bare credal statement that Jesus died for our sins, or that he died to save us from the power of death.

Most college students I have met are willing to assent to such credal statements, but they also generally find them irrelevant to their lives. They, like many others, will probably continue to hold them because it does not cost anything to do so. They have simply inherited the Catholic liturgical and doctrinal rhetoric of their families and teachers. What has happened is that the New Testament writers (and the subsequent tradition) have reflected long and hard on the death of Jesus. Woven into the gospel narratives, together with clues as to the historical events surrounding the life and death of Jesus, is an evolving reflection, born of faith and born also from the practice of discipleship. But to present people with the reflection and the developed faith that comes from years of believing in and following Jesus, before they have had an opportunity to consider the experience and history behind that faith, is to render them a disservice; one might be asking too much of them. Such faith has not been tested by an encounter with the real Jesus. Somehow, each Christian has to be drawn into the gospel episodes where people react to Jesus, in order to bring to light how his message, his actions and his person put our lives on trial. Our reactions, after all, could prove to be very similar to, say, the reaction of the scribes and Pharisees, or the townspeople of Nazareth, or the rich man of Mark 10, or John the Baptist languishing in Herod's dungeon (Lk 7:18–23), or even to the disciples themselves, who, upon Jesus' arrest, fell apart. Jesus offended many people. There is no reason to doubt that he would have offended us, too, by failing to meet our expectations, or by embodying an inner freedom which would threaten us to the core of our souls. A person truly liberated is dangerous; life in the Spirit, the day-to-day existence of one who is truly a daughter or son of God, is subversive.

This may explain why a book like Segundo's proves so valuable. It tries to put its readers in touch with the concrete circumstances in which Jesus lived and moved, and in which people were deciding for and against him. The stakes involved were much higher than the everyday concerns in the life of a typical undergraduate, or indeed, than the concerns of those in the mainstream of life in the developed countries. Jesus was not crucified simply because he healed paralytics or drove out "evil spirits" on the sabbath, or even because, as a layman, he forgave sins in God's name. These things may be the stuff of the controversies which the evangelists have recorded, but such controversies almost certainly reflect the conflict and tension of the evangelists' day, rather than what took place at the time of Jesus.

Whatever their scholarly limitations, works such as Leonardo Boff's *Jesus Christ Liberator* or Jon Sobrino's *Christology at the Crossroads* are likewise helpful in sharpening the issues which Jesus preached about and defended, and for which he was finally crucified. Again, they are not easy reading (Sobrino less so than Boff), yet we do learn something from them about the intrinsic link between believing and doing, or faith and justice, in Jesus' ministry. Another work which illumines considerably the political background of Jesus' life is Richard

Horsley's *Jesus and the Spiral of Violence*. In his book *The Historical Jesus: The Life of a Mediterranean Jewish Peasant*, John Dominic Crossan locates Jesus in the Galilean countryside and brings his political and social worlds to life with an abundance of detail, although the reading is somewhat dense and the theological slant angular; the story of Jesus is reconstructed apart from the experience of God behind it. Yet all of these studies illustrate why the political dimensions of the gospel narrative need to be fleshed out, if the full scope of God's saving action in Jesus is to be appreciated.

Salvation Has Social and Economic Dimensions

One of the features which especially commends liberation theology to us as we endeavor to immerse ourselves in the gospel story is the situation from which the Latin Americans write. There the voice of the poor has truly called out to the rest of the world. Their experience resonates with large portions of the experience of God's people over the centuries, starting with the foundational biblical memory of slavery and oppression in Egypt. This present-day experience becomes the key by which one reads or interprets the action of God in history which we call redemption or salvation. God's salvation, the argument goes, cannot be divorced from the real, concrete things from which human beings need to be saved. To say that God has saved us from our sins is all well and good, but most people who experience themselves as heavily burdened are suffering from other things, too, and given the chance, they would give their right arm to stand before God, like Job, and plead their case. To be sure, sin and guilt are things from which men and women of faith want to be released; one has only to glance through the Psalms to appreciate this. Yet it is hard to imagine that the first thing someone who has been paralyzed for a long time, or who is blind, or who is afflicted with leprosy, would ask God for, given the opportunity, is forgiveness from his or her sins. That may indeed be the thing they most need from God (which would likewise be true for all of us), but it is unlikely that forgiveness would be the first need to leap to mind.

There is an early episode in Mark where this is exactly what is reported. A paralyzed man is let down through the roof, presumably into the middle of Peter's house, and Jesus says, "Child, your sins are forgiven." Actually, this is the only incident of its kind in Mark. There is an episode in John's gospel also involving a paralyzed man, where Jesus' last words to him are, "Look, you are well now; do not sin any more, so that nothing worse may happen to you" (Jn 5:14). Yet these incidents should not mislead us into thinking that physical healing was automatically linked to the forgiveness of sins. Indeed, the mistaken idea did circulate among some in Jesus' day that physical infirmity was the result of an individual's sin. If that was the case in these two incidents, then we can understand Jesus' hastening to reassure people of divine forgiveness. But Jesus would not have subscribed to this idea; the God he experienced as Father did not afflict men and women with disease and infirmity in order to punish them for their sins. If anything, then, Jesus' manner in the scene from Mark brings to the fore the reality and accessibility of divine mercy and compassion, precisely in contrast to those who would in any way restrict the availability of divine forgiveness, or confine it to the rituals of religion, or make it contingent upon acts of penance.

With this clarification in mind, we return to the main point that God's saving action on our behalf extends as much to the political, social and economic realities of human life as it does to the inner or spiritual reality of human sinfulness and guilt. While they would not have employed some of the categories we might use as we talk about institutional sin or structural violence, they certainly felt the effects of injustice. Again, it would be impossible to conceive that Jesus could have carried on his ministry without adverting to or addressing the problems which oppressed people. He spoke about God; there is no doubt about that. But he did not incur enemies because he was teaching children how to pray, or because he was catechizing adults, or even because he occasionally healed people. Jesus brought God into the everyday world and its concerns. Foreign soldiers were policing the land, which was being taxed into submission by a pagan empire. Young people suspected of revolutionary fervor could be summarily executed. One of the infancy stories recounts King Herod's brutal murder of innocent children, and the gospels also report the arrest and murder of John the Baptist by another Herod. Much more could be said, but the bottom line is that there was violence and repression in the land: that was the historical situation.

What Prompted Jesus to Begin His Mission

Mark devotes considerable space in chapter six to the death of John the Baptist, and fittingly so. John was the great prophet, Elijah-like in stature, even the greatest among those born of women (Mt 11:11), whose message and spirit had made a strong impact on Jesus. Jesus, Mark informs us, had begun his ministry after John was arrested (1:14). Now, this piece of information can be taken in several ways. It might simply be a stage direction: exit John, enter Jesus. In order for Jesus to operate without any "competition" from John, John needs to be off the scene. The transition between the old wineskins and new wine thus becomes clear. The relevant footnote in *The Catholic Study Bible* adopts this interpretation: "In the plan of God, Jesus was not to proclaim the good news of salvation prior to the termination of the Baptist's active mission." This way of viewing things, however, inserts a passive note into the gospel story, as if Jesus were obediently following a script instead of actively responding to the events of his day in sound prophetic fashion.

But the sense of Mark's phrase might be causal rather than temporal: *because* John was arrested, or *as a result of* John's arrest, Jesus went public and he came to Galilee proclaiming the time of fulfillment. This suggestion, if the authors of *Un tal Jesus* are on the right track, casts a more obviously political hue over the beginning of Jesus' public ministry. Might Jesus have been outraged by the news that John, the great prophet, under whose cleansing hands Jesus himself had undergone an extraordinary religious experience, had been arrested? Might he have thought that the message of John must at all costs continue to be preached (even if the message would be reshaped in terms of Jesus' own understanding of the kingdom of God)? In short, was the arrest of John the catalyst for Jesus' decision to speak out? And if so, is it likely that Jesus would have had no public comment to make about John, about his arrest and about the cruel and unjust tyrant whose consort John had offended?

Again, it is inconceivable that Jesus could have ignored these political events in his own preaching and conversation, since everyone would have heard and started talking about them. And later, when the news broke that Herod had beheaded John, surely Jesus would have had something to say to the people: if John had the prophetic courage to stand up to the political power of Galilee and denounce his immoral behavior in public, certainly Jesus would not have been afraid to do the same. Isn't it likely, then, that Jesus would have attacked Herod for murdering one of God's prophets? And if he spoke out on this matter, is it probable that he would have kept silent about other matters which would have prompted those in power to notice him? Otherwise, how are we to we explain the caution given to Jesus by some Pharisees (in this case, presumably friendly ones), "Go away, leave this area because Herod wants to kill you"? To which Jesus boldly replied, "Go and tell that fox . . ." (Lk 13:31–32). The views of Jesus would have been sufficiently well-known to Herod's police that Jesus stood in danger of being arrested. Needless to say, he had no kind words for the likes of Herod.

14

The Eyes of a Prophet

"The lamp of the body is the eye. If your eye is sound, your whole body will be filled with light; but if your eye is bad, your whole body will be in darkness" (Mt 6:22–23).

One of the lessons of literary studies and social analyses in the twentieth century is that one must be alert, critical, even suspicious when it comes to reading texts, or reading people and events, for that matter. What meets the eye may not always be the meaning intended by the text, and the reason that the eye often misses the intended meaning of things may be that a person's experience of life and of the world has narrowed the field of vision so as to render the truth opaque. I remember once describing to a university professor the background of several teenagers I had met. Both had been abandoned by their fathers. Both came from families with long histories of drug addiction, alcoholism, relatives in and out of prison, living in public shelters, and public welfare. Unbeknownst to one of them, his mother was dying of AIDS; he himself had been a drug-addicted infant. The professor summed things up, "Yes, I suppose there are lots of kids around who are down on their luck!" "Down on their luck!", I stammered to myself. "When had they ever been lucky in the first place?" It is seldom easy for those of us with access to the refinements of culture to appreciate the position others are coming from.

One needs to be suspicious about reality; things are often not what they seem. When people who are really poor and "down on their luck" wind up in prison, one should not automatically assume that poor, uneducated people have more criminal tendencies than the rest of human beings. Social and economic factors deeply influence behavior, which is not something which was always adverted to and understood. The fact that people turn to crime is not unrelated to the pent-up frustration and feelings of impotence which those at the bottom of the social ladder experience. Of course, those who are poor, marginalized, or at the bottom of the social ladder are by no means automatically outlaws. That is why Jesus reacted very differently to the "prostitutes" and "tax-collectors" than many righteous people did. He saw beyond their social class and their "crimes," and recognized them as his brothers and sisters, for that is what they were. Because he beheld the world through God's eyes, Jesus had broken through stereotypes; he saw reality as it was.

One can read a text but miss its underlying meaning. I believe that there are two reasons for this kind of oversight when it comes to reading the Bible. First, the tradition which handed the gospel story down to us has failed to internalize an important attitude of Jesus. And second, those at the top of the social ladder often fail to comprehend the situation of those at the bottom. Like the rich man who dressed in purple garments and fine linen, they fail even to notice what lies outside their door. Two gospel texts illustrate this rather effectively.

The Exploited Widow

The first text is that of the poor widow who put the two small coins into the temple treasury, "all she had, her whole livelihood" (Mk 12:44). Most of us have been accustomed to hearing this text as an endorsement of generous giving, especially to religious causes. If the poor widow could contribute all she had, then we who possess much more can afford to donate considerably, until it hurts. The widow becomes the patron saint of religious fund-raisers, and Jesus becomes her promoter.

This text, however, is sandwiched between Jesus' denouncing the scribes who "devour the houses of widows" (Mk 12:4), and his prediction about the destruction of the temple: "There will not be one stone left upon another that will not be thrown down" (13:2). There is something queer about all of this. Why would Jesus commend the widow's giving to the temple treasury (presumably for the upkeep of the temple) in view of its impending destruction? The answer is that Jesus does not actually approve of the widow's action; he merely makes an observation. Admittedly, Jesus' sympathies are with the woman, and not with the many rich people. But the attitude of Jesus here would more appropriately be anger than anything else, especially since he has just expressed outrage over the scribes who devour widows' homes. They do this, apparently, not by literally eating poor women out of house and home, but rather by cultivating in such defenseless people the erroneous idea that generosity of this sort is what God wants. Blind guides have misled poor people into believing that God is pleased when they give all they have, even their whole livelihood, to the temple treasury. Undoubtedly, in her own mind, the widow has performed a sacrifice. But, looking at things from Jesus' standpoint, she has been manipulated by religious leaders into doing something which, objectively, is anything but pleasing to God. What merit is there in going hungry? Is this what God desires *of the poor*? "In short, Jesus' comment contains words of lament, not of praise" (see Joseph Fitzmyer, *The Gospel According to Luke x–xxiv* [Doubleday & Co., 1985], p. 1321).

When read together with the texts which precede and follow it, this passage about the widow carries an altogether different meaning from the one which the tradition has passed along as it praised "the widow's mite." It turns into a story about abuse, and it highlights once more the nature of Jesus' confrontations with those occupying positions of power over their sisters and brothers. There should have been some suspicion, somewhere along the line, that if Jesus had been commending the widow's action, then he would have been behaving out of character. Jesus had no vested interest in the upkeep of the temple. The text's prophetic meaning remained hidden, perhaps because the church lost sight of the sort of person Jesus really was, or perhaps because, not being in the situation of the defenseless widow, church leaders and teachers had little sense of how reality feels from the underside of history, or from the bottom of the social ladder. What sort of God did the widow need to hear about? What would have been good news for her?

God, Caesar and Money

The second text is that of the trick question from some Pharisees and Herodians about whether it was right to pay taxes to the emperor (Mk 12:13–17). The answer about rendering to Caesar what is Caesar's, and to God what is God's, appears quite subtle. If subtlety was indeed the issue, then Jesus' response was truly cause for astonishment.

God and Caesar are not parallels, like two sides of a balance. Caesar is everything God is not. The saying about not serving God and money is relevant here (Mt 6:24), because it is Caesar's image which appears on the Roman coin. In other words, Caesar represents money. Furthermore, Jesus does not have a coin; his adversaries have to produce one and show it to him, which forces them to place Caesar's image and inscription in the palm of their hand, something which should have been abhorrent to anyone serious about obeying the divine prohibition against graven images. Caesar is a false God. The "render to Caesar," therefore, makes better sense if it does not mean that Jesus is approving the payment of taxes. After all, how could he? Not only would such an endorsement on his part be terribly imprudent, since through it he would forfeit whatever popular support he had; it would also be out of character. What interest does Jesus have in the paying of imperial taxes? He would have no more interest in that than he would in settling an inheritance dispute (Lk 12:13–14).

In the same vein, the Mexican theologian José Miranda made a tempting suggestion about this text. The sense of "render to Caesar" ought to be "Give back to garbage what belongs to garbage." God's real rival, Miranda argued, is money. Jesus, who has already insisted that we cannot serve them both, is presented with a Roman coin, which at that moment embodies all civil authority. Returning the money to the government, therefore, would be tantamount to radically undercutting all political authority, a point which would not have been lost on the crowd around Jesus. Thus Jesus' answer becomes sarcastic rather than shrewd. Miranda's proposal may appear to be stretching the text, but it sounds far more like the answer of a prophet than of an ecclesiastical lawyer (*Communism in the Bible* [Orbis Books, 1982], pg. 64–65) .

This text, too, has served an ideological purpose over the course of the Christian tradition. Jesus has been viewed as supporting the notion that Christians should be good citizens, that they should obey God in what belongs to God and obey the state in what is proper to the state. Perhaps the idea received an influx of energy as the church increasingly viewed Jesus as exalted Lord, and neglected to meditate sufficiently upon his humble origins. Or perhaps the trouble arose when bishops began consorting with emperors. For not only did the church elevate Jesus to be Caesar's equal in terms of power and prestige; Jesus also surpassed him in precisely those categories where Caesar was regarded to be important. Yet the very idea that Jesus could have sanctioned splitting allegiances between God and the state is unthinkable; indeed, doing so would have been idolatrous. There is nothing Caesar had that Jesus would have wanted to be associated with: neither money, nor power, nor lordship over others, nor military might, nor prestige, nor the claim to be divine. The reason why this text's revolutionary meaning escaped us for so long, therefore, is that we lost touch with the whole Jesus story. This goes beyond the interpretation given by one of the standard commentaries on Mark:

> To understand Jesus' words here we must keep in mind his conviction that the future of this world, and of the Roman empire within it, would be short; very soon the kingdom of heaven would arrive and the rule of Rome would disappear, not through man's agency but through God's. Essentially, therefore, Jesus is not enunciating any principle bearing on the problem of "Church and State" . . . he is saying simply that men's duty to Caesar does not contradict their duty to God; it is insignificant in comparison with it (D. E. Nineham, *Saint Mark* [Penguin Books, 1963], pp. 315–16).

However subtle Jesus' response may sound, the likely fact is that people knew very well what his opinion of Caesar was. Otherwise, the title "prophet" would have been totally undeserved. The effort of religious leaders to bait Jesus into imperial quicksand would have been pointless, if Jesus had never been known to address himself to the political and social affairs of his time.

According to the great commandment, the primary form of idolatry is not so much the worship of idols, but the elevation of some finite thing into the sanctuary of one's soul. The text reads: "Therefore, you shall love the Lord, your God, with all your heart, and with all your soul, and with all your strength" (Deut 6:5). The point of the text becomes all the stronger if we interpret it to be a definition of God rather than an instruction or a command. By definition our God is going to be whatever we serve with all our heart, mind and strength. The divine injunction, therefore, is that we make sure that the God we love is nothing less than the one true God: God the Creator, the God who called the people of Israel into being, the God who liberates and makes promises.

In practice, however, what many people really love and devote themselves to is money (hence Jesus' statement that we simply cannot serve two masters, God and money); together with the love of power, this is one of the primary forms of idol worship. Idolatry makes a person deaf to God. The failure of the ruling elites to hear and respond to Jesus, as this episode about the coin of tribute shows, results from their idolatry. The fact is that they really worshipped money; they would try to make money even at the expense of poor widows. Therefore, they could never hear God's voice behind Jesus' words. Never.

15

Understanding the Meaning of the Loaves

One book which opens up its readers rather quickly to the human side of the gospel story is Albert Nolan's *Jesus Before Christianity*. And one of the particularly intriguing insights from the book is Nolan's account of the multiplication of the loaves and fishes. Although I resisted his view initially, after a number of semesters I found myself more and more persuaded by its inner reasonableness, despite Raymond Brown's admonition:

> Yet, I warn very strongly against a modernization of the miracles in liberal fashion, e.g., explaining the multiplication of the loaves in terms of Jesus touching the hearts of those present so that they opened their knapsacks and brought out hidden food. That is absolute nonsense: it is not what the Gospels narrate, but rather an attempt to evade the import of what is narrated (*Responses to 101 Questions on the Bible*, p. 67).

One will have to decide for oneself whether Nolan's point evades the text's import: "But the event itself was not a miracle of multiplication; it was a remarkable example of sharing" (Nolan, p. 51). And again: "The 'miracle' was that so many men should suddenly cease to be possessive about their food and begin to share, only to discover that there was enough to go around" (Nolan, p. 52).

The gospel account of the multiplication of the loaves is one with which everyone is familiar, if not from reading the gospel text or hearing it read in church, then maybe from seeing its dramatic cinematic rendering in Zeffirelli's *Jesus of Nazareth*. The scene is reminiscent of God's feeding the people of Israel with manna in the wilderness (Ex 16). The parallel would probably not have been sharpened by Jesus himself, however, but by the early communities which told and retold the story. It would be stretching things to insinuate that Jesus consciously envisioned himself reenacting the event of God's feeding the people of Israel in the desert.

The first question we might raise is this: Is it likely that such a large crowd of men (not to mention the women and children [Mt 14:21]) would have gone to a "deserted place" without thinking about bringing something along to eat? Were they counting on local fast-food shops? Even if the men, in their eagerness to catch up with Jesus and his disciples, had left their homes in so much haste, surely their wives would have had enough presence of mind to bring along some provisions, especially if they had taken along their children! True, the evangelists do not tell us that the crowds had actually brought food with them, but according to John's account, one young boy at least had apparently not forgotten that he might get hungry (Jn 6:9); someone had the common sense to pack a lunch of a few loaves and fishes before setting out to find Jesus. One could imagine that many others would also have brought food, but seeing the multitude around them, and fearing that their neighbors might not have been as forethoughtful, they kept their provisions hidden. Without some signal from Jesus that would have freed them to share their food with one another, the crowds most likely would have trailed off, nibbling their bread and olives, dates and figs, as they made their way home.

We have to wonder, then, what the more compelling kingdom sign would have been: a miraculous multiplying of loaves from otherwise empty baskets (for apparently there were at least a dozen baskets or hampers around to collect the leftovers [Mk 6:43]), or the breaking down of fear and greed which might lead people to hoard food and possessions, and prevent them from seeing others, who had likewise come to hear the word of God, as their true family? Indeed, the first alternative would send a clear signal that Jesus himself was God's prophet, on a par with Moses. It would suggest God's dramatic intervention into their life and times, as had happened to their ancestors in the wilderness.

But the second alternative is more serviceable for the future. The second sends quite a different signal: God is not going to fill, in miraculous fashion, family breadbaskets left on the doorstep overnight (not even the breadbaskets of the poor), but God can open human hearts so that people begin to attend to one another's needs and to share with each other even the little that they have. While the text does not state this explicitly, it certainly does not rule out that this might be the real meaning of Jesus' actions. It is also more eucharistic, because such a reconstruction emphasizes the action of breaking and sharing (or sacrificing and giving) over the material substance of bread. Christ's real presence in the bread, in other words, would be rendered useless, unless his community was prepared to lay aside all greed and fear, and to share with their brothers and sisters in need. Indeed, the "liberationist" reading of the passage makes the episode much more real than the "miraculous" reading. As I mentioned, I resisted this possibility the first time I read of it; but from the side of the poor, the story of the loaves would be just another case of the God of the upper classes intervening in the nick of time. Such a God does not empower anyone, let alone the poor.

The Narrative Effect of Doubling the Story

The fact that the story is recounted twice underscores the liberationist reading. Apart from whatever scribal explanations might be adduced, the duplication of the episode, from a storyteller's viewpoint, makes considerable sense. Mark tells us the story in 6:34–44, and then he narrates the miraculous feeding of a crowd four thousand strong in 8:1–10. No doubt, from his perspective Jesus had worked a great wonder; the Jesus who could perform such a miracle could just as surely walk on water (6:52). Now, it is hardly news that the disciples in Mark are constantly misunderstanding Jesus. Even so, the fact that they could be in the same situation a second time (and so soon), and a second time ask, "Where can anyone get enough bread to satisfy them here in this deserted place?" (8:4), forces us to conclude that the disciples of Jesus had to be a bunch of morons. Mark's observation that the disciples had misunderstood the meaning of the loaves the first time because "their hearts were hardened" (6:52) might be more comprehensible if we conjecture that the real hardening was a matter of hardened wallets: "Are we to buy two hundred days' wages worth of food and give it to them to eat?" (6:37). The disciples had failed (or refused) to grasp the lesson about sharing. Yet sharing would lie at the heart of the experience of the kingdom. Until and unless men and women could open their homes and their hearts, nothing was going to change. In the kingdom there was no room for fear and greed.

The second episode similarly is followed by a case of misunderstanding. The disciples had only one loaf of bread in the boat. When Jesus warned them, "Watch out, guard against the leaven of the Pharisees and the leaven of Herod" (8:15), they figured he was referring to bread. Not only were they unable to perceive the metaphorical meaning of Jesus' words; they had probably fallen into arguing about whose fault it was that they had failed to bring any food along. Jesus then rebukes the whole bunch, and reminds them about what they had twice witnessed. The implication would appear to be that if Jesus could multiply loaves for the crowds, he could certainly do the same in order to feed himself and his disciples.

But Jesus never worked miracles on his own behalf. I would suggest, therefore, that his irritation came not from the fact that his disciples could not latch onto the idea that Jesus truly had power to work miracles. Rather, it came from the fact that they were greedy, quarrelsome and fearful. It would accomplish nothing if Jesus assured them, each time they were in dire straits, that he would provide for their needs. Such an approach on his part would have made them dependent upon God in an immature way: God (or Jesus) would always be there to satisfy their wants. This, of course, is simply not our experience of God; nor could it have been theirs. The problem was not getting God (or Jesus) to provide whenever they might find themselves alone, adrift, or without food; the problem was that their hearts had not changed:

> "Do you not yet understand or comprehend? Are your hearts hardened? Do you have eyes and not see, ears and not hear? And do you not remember?" (Mk 8:17–18)

One way in which the liberating action of God shows itself consists in the empowering of human beings to do things for themselves, together, as brothers and sisters. The God of Jesus is not so much above the world, directing and providing. The God of Jesus is among us, walking alongside, as our fellow-traveler through history, liberating men and women from the fears, the prejudices and the greed which keep them apart.

The younger generation of believers responds warmly to this interpretation. They do so, not because they reject the very possibility of miracles; in this, they are not like eighteenth-century rationalists, or twentieth-century agnostics. Their positive response comes from the fact that the explanation itself sounds more sensible. If the "miracle" or "sign" which Jesus performed requires knowledge of the symbolic background of the event, if it is laden with various levels of hidden meaning, then they do not find themselves particularly moved by it, although they appreciate the background information. If the feeding was miraculous in the traditional sense, then the miracle is relevant only to the people before whom it took place. It cannot even be viewed as a protest against hunger, since the hunger of the people was not the pernicious hunger associated with prolonged poverty, but the temporary hunger of people who found themselves stranded and imprudent, because they had failed to bring along provisions. Since the miraculous feeding is hardly a banquet scene (the fare was rather simple), the miracle does not reveal the extravagance of the kingdom of God, either. The only other messages it might convey, therefore, would have to do with the identity of Jesus as a second Moses, or as a wonder-worker. And as I remarked, while this may be interesting, symbolic association is not going to draw attention to the miraculous way hearts have to change.

The story of the loaves, as recounted by the evangelists, has certainly acquired a christological focus, that is, it concentrates on the person and power of Jesus. The actual episode, in the eyes of Jesus, should have focussed people's attention on the meaning of the kingdom, for everything he did pointed to that new reality. The connection between these two moments (which was clear to the gospel writers but often missed by those preoccupied with the identity of Jesus as God's Son) is that the kingdom possibilities envisioned and preached by Jesus would become inseparable from his enduring presence among his disciples throughout the ages.

16

Blessings and Woes

For many people, the quintessentially Christian texts in the New Testament are the Lord's Prayer and the Beatitudes. The prayer can be found in Matthew 6:9–13 and Luke 11:2–4; the Beatitudes are given in Matthew 5:3–12 and Luke 6:20–23 (Lk 6:24–26 parallels the four blessings with four woes). In each version of the prayer there are four basic requests addressed to God: that God would usher in the kingdom, or the rule of God on earth; that God would ensure that we have sufficient food for the day; that God would forgive whatever sins or faults we have; and that God would spare us by not letting us fall in that severe and final trial which, people of Jesus' day believed, would come just before the end of time. For all practical purposes, however, there are three petitions here: for the kingdom, for daily bread, and for forgiveness. These petitions correspond to three great human needs: for justice in the world, for an end to hunger, and for the reconciliation among human beings which will at last make a truly humanized world community possible.

According to the spirit of the prayer, none of these needs can be met by human resourcefulness alone; we depend for their fulfillment upon the grace and mercy of God. That is why the kingdom of God (or whatever reality corresponds to that biblical expression) is always viewed as divine gift, the content of God's promise to Israel and, through the people of Israel, to the whole human race. Strictly speaking, human beings do not build the kingdom; they receive it. It comes as pure gift, that is, as the Spirit's response to our openness to the reality of God in our lives. This opening of oneself to God is just another way of describing the process of repentance and conversion, which explains why Jesus began his prophetic career by proclaiming,

"The kingdom of God is at hand. *Repent, and believe in the gospel*" (Mk 1:15). In the kingdom of God, no one will want for food, nor will anger, resentment, suspicion and hatred keep brothers and sisters apart.

Clearly, the Lord's Prayer is a kingdom prayer. It was formulated by someone for whom the kingdom of God was both a passionate hope and a driving concern. The great promise of God was redemption and liberation; the great hope of the people, based on that promise, was the transformation of the world and human society here and now so that justice, reconciliation and community prevailed. But everything hinged upon human response; men and women had to prepare themselves for this new reality through repentance and faith. They had to believe that this new reality was indeed possible. It might have a small, humble beginning in individuals and families; it could spread to neighborhoods and villages; it could sprout far and wide across the country, and it could one day appear all over the earth. First, however, men and women had to want it. They needed to desire it more than they desired anything else, and they needed to be prepared to lay aside everything which might stand in the way of the kingdom's advent.

The Terms of the Kingdom

Yet the sad fact was that, while many people would have welcomed the kingdom, they did not welcome it along the lines drawn by Jesus. The kingdom of God was inclusive, for the invitation had been addressed to all, even, eventually, to people outside the nation of Israel. Many, of course, would have bristled at this. And many within Israel itself were going to have to renounce whatever prejudices, attachments and loyalties divided men and women, and prevented their seeing one another as family. The decisive intervention of God in history was not about to happen without human cooperation, and part of that cooperation would consist of redefining who was rich and who was poor in God's sight. No one could be one with God in the Spirit who did not share God's vision and outlook; the test as to whether or not one shared that vision was whether one could sit down at God's table with the other guests whom God had likewise invited. A person whose pantry was filled with provisions, whose barns were overflowing, and whose herds were rich with milk, would have had a hard time honestly praying, "Give us the bread we need to carry us through this day" or "Give us the strength to toil hard so that we might earn enough to buy bread for our families."

In the same way, a person who never bothered to examine the inequalities which existed among men and women and who never perceived the evils which drove human beings apart would have had a hard time measuring the meaning of the words "for we ourselves forgive everyone in debt to us" (Lk 11:4). What, one has to ask, are those debts? Is Jesus referring to the insults and lies, the gossip, anger and slander which human beings direct against one another? Or is he speaking about real debts, about those arrangements which put one human being in a disadvantageous financial situation with respect to another *who is also his brother or sister?* When we ask God to forgive us our "debts," naturally the first thing which comes to our minds is our sins; that is how we have been accustomed to hearing it. But in what way does sin make us indebted to God? One could only be in God's debt *after* receiving the grace of forgiveness. Doesn't it make better gospel sense to suggest that every human being is automatically in debt to God, not on account of sin, but because God has already given us everything that we have?

The Meaning of Being in Debt

Perhaps the best commentary on the meaning of such indebtedness is Jesus' parable about the unforgiving servant (Mt 18:21–35). When Jesus wanted to explain what it meant to forgive one's brother from the bottom of his heart he told a story about a servant who owed his king a large amount of money. Upon listening to the pleading of his servant, the king was "moved with compassion" and canceled or forgave the loan, which, we are told, was an enormous amount of money. Of course, in our own day, people are not so much indebted to one another as they are to their banks, and thus the cutting edge of the parable misses our experience. It thus becomes too easy to substitute "sin" or "trespass" for "debt."

Yet the fact is that from God's side all of us are in debt because none of us would have been able to draw a single breath of air unless God had first advanced us the creature's capital, which is life itself. None of us would have been able to set foot upon the earth, unless

God, the earth's only real owner, had permitted us to do so. Each of us, therefore, already owes God so huge an amount that there is simply no way we could ever repay what has been loaned to us *except* by treating our brothers and sisters with that same generosity which God has showed toward us. Forgiveness, in other words, is what God requires as our repayment for all that has been given to us.

Now, having given us such a parable to illustrate what forgiveness means, it would make little sense for Jesus to exclude from the category of debt the very real financial burdens which keep people poor, because whatever financial structures or institutions keep poor people poor are in and of themselves evil. The disciple who prays the *Lord's* prayer must possess the attitude of the kingdom: in God's sight all are debtors, and the only way to have that debt removed is to treat one's brothers and sisters with consummate justice and generosity. Whatever forces them to become, literally, indebted to us so that they lose their dignity or compromise their independence is evil. Thus Richard Horsley observes, "the petition about 'forgiveness' presupposes that the people had already forgiven one another in their local social-economic relations" (*Jesus and the Spiral of Violence*, p. 254).

The person who first formulated this prayer was apparently looking at life from the underside of history. The petitions enshrined in the prayer were meant to be heard and answered by God literally, not metaphorically: justice, food, freedom from debt. Those of us who approach history from the topside, as it were, bolstered by all the advantages of living comfortably and securely, tend to spiritualize the intention of the prayer. The bread requested for each day might be eucharistic bread. The kingdom is the heavenly reward for the righteous. The forgiveness of debts becomes the remission of sins. Those on the top do not require a great deal from God, and therefore they ask little. Only when those on the top begin to look at the world through the eyes of those at the bottom will the Lord's Prayer start to recover its radical, revolutionary hope. One cannot pray the prayer of Jesus, any more than one can pray with the spirit of Jesus, unless one shares Jesus' faith and prophetic, revolutionary outlook. The God who will bring about the kingdom is also the God who tumbles rulers from their thrones and drives the rich away empty (Lk 1:52–53). To ask God, therefore, to hasten the advent of the kingdom is at the same time to ask God to transform the face of society by unseating the rich and the powerful from their positions of control. Needless to say, there are

many things which Christians may want to ask God for besides the
concerns embodied in the Lord's Prayer, but to pray with the spirit of
Jesus presupposes at the very least that we have first shared and voiced
those concerns which mattered most to him.

The Blessings

The radical perspective of the Lord's Prayer likewise appears in the
Beatitudes. For the sake of simplicity, let us follow Luke's version:

> Blessed are you who are poor,
>   for the kingdom of God is yours.
> Blessed are you who are now hungry,
>   for you will be satisfied.
> Blessed are you who are now weeping,
>   for you will laugh.
> Blessed are you when people hate you,
>   and when they exclude and insult you,
>   and denounce your name as evil
>   on account of the Son of Man. (Lk 6:20–22)

Connected to the fourth blessing is the cause for rejoicing: "Rejoice
and leap for joy! Behold your reward will be great in heaven. For their
ancestors treated the prophets in the same way" (6:23).

Although the point is obvious, nevertheless it should be remarked
that what Jesus has pronounced "blessed" or "favored by God" is not the
condition of the poor: being poor is not a blessing, any more than being
hungry, or hated and denounced, or mournful would be. (We should
take those "who are now weeping" to refer to the pain and distress
engendered by poverty: people weep because they have no food to give
their children, or because they lose an infant to hunger or disease, or
because, lacking any means of defense, they suffer from having their
rights denied or wages withheld, from seeing their sons and daughters
unjustly accused, imprisoned, and tortured, or because they have no
resources to move their families from a dangerous neighborhood.
These are the sorts of things which cause people to weep and to mourn,
and, clearly, being condemned to such a condition is hardly a blessing). What leads Jesus to pronounce such people "blessed" is his abso-

lute conviction that God has taken the side of men and women like these. They belong to God in a most special way, and it has pleased God to champion their cause. To them belongs the kingdom; divine justice itself guarantees it. In the great restoration, when all of society is changed from the bottom up, those who have turned to God in faith and hope (since there really is no other place to turn) will find justice, and food, and laughter.

On the other side, however, there are the ones who have had it all:

> But woe to you who are rich,
>   for you have received your consolation.
> But woe to you who are filled now,
>   for you will be hungry.
> Woe to you who laugh now,
>   for you will grieve and weep.
> Woe to you when all speak well of you,
>   for their ancestors treated the false
>   prophets in this way. (Lk 6:24–26)

The contrasting "woes" highlight a striking feature of the parallel: just as the condition of being poor is not a blessing, neither is being rich. Just as the condition of being hungry is hardly a blessing, neither is the condition of "being filled," or of being well received by everybody (because one poses no threat to anyone's interests, or because one lacks the integrity to speak the truth). Those occupying positions of power and authority which set them over and above others, thereby generating the outrageous differences between those who have and those who do not have, are going to have to face the frightening prospect of having their sources of power and security ripped out of their hands.

For Jesus, God is not about merely to alter things so that the rich and the poor trade places, which ultimately solves nothing. God is about to eliminate the present structure of reality altogether. The poor are not going to become rich overnight; in the kingdom, the root of the imbalance between rich and poor will be done away with. In the new order of things, those unjustly accused and condemned are not suddenly going to find themselves made judges, while their former adversaries become a new class of victims. That is hardly the way Jesus interpreted the fulfillment of the divine promise to liberate. Yet there should be no mistaking the fact that the kingdom is going to separate the rich from their wealth and their power, for as long as these things exist men and women will remain unable fully to see one another as sisters and brothers.

The Spirit Behind the Beatitudes Is the Spirit of the Prophets

In his commentary on Matthew's gospel, Daniel Harrington writes:

> The Beatitudes are often presented in preaching and teaching as Jesus' distinctive contribution to defining the elements of good character or as a list of Jesus' values in opposition to those of the world. Or they are sometimes taken as part of an "ethics of discipleship" intended only for those who follow Jesus already. But the Beatitudes are neither philosophical nor sectarian ethics. The Beatitudes are thoroughly Jewish in form and content. They challenged those who made up "Israel" in Matthew's time by delineating the kinds of persons and actions that will receive their full reward when the kingdom comes. They remind Christians today of the Jewish roots of their piety and challenge each generation to reflect on what persons and actions they consider to be important or "blessed" (*The Gospel of Matthew*, p. 84).

That Jesus is not simply imparting a code of moral norms, or that he has not devised a distinctively "Christian" philosophy of life through the Beatitudes, is extremely important to note. Throughout this gospel text, Jesus proves himself to be in continuity with the hope of Israel concerning God's faithfulness to the divine promise. The Beatitudes confirm all that we know about the divine sensitivity to the voice of those who are defenseless and poor, and they are thoroughly consistent with what one would expect a prophet of Israel to teach. In short, there is nothing sweet and consoling about them. If one is rich, the Beatitudes are not good news. If one is poor, they are more likely to be heard as prophetic protests against the way things are. Whatever consolation one hears in them, from the side of the poor, has to do with the reconfirmation of one's hope in the enduring promise of God.

The reason for reflecting this way, and for moving outside the gospel of Mark at this point, is that Mark does not tell us a great deal about what Jesus actually taught. Yet, if Jesus is a prophet of Israel, in continuity with the prophetic spirit of the tradition, then his concerns would have been on a number of key points like theirs. What Matthew and Luke have elaborated could just as easily have been placed on Jesus' lips by Mark, especially the attitude we find in the Lord's Prayer and the Beatitudes. The two guiding questions I proposed at the outset were: "Who is Jesus?" and "What would I be prepared to do along with him for the sake of the kingdom of God?" Maybe at this point it is well worth asking ourselves who Jesus is. Who is the man who teaches what we have seen here? What was on his mind? What were his burning concerns? And as these come into view ever more sharply, we have to examine ourselves. Would we be willing to stand with him, not only in his teaching, but also in his witness to justice?

Exclusion, insult, hatred, denunciation: this is what greeted the prophets of old. The same things await those who stand with Jesus, the Son of man. We might prefer a soft and gentle Jesus. We might feel safer if Jesus, like a kindly professor or philosopher, merely imparted noble truths. We might even consider ourselves sufficiently distinctive if Jesus had simply proposed a set of enlightened ethical principles for us to live by. But to cross the line into witness and action: that might be another matter entirely. To find the motivation and strength to do so, we have to recapture the spirit behind the Lord's own prayer, and the Beatitudes. There we find the critical message, which lies just below the surface in Mark's gospel, and which accounts all the more for why those in positions of power considered him a threat.

17

Two Tales about Jesus

Mark was a consummate storyteller. The first evangelist wove memories and traditions about Jesus together with the passion narrative in order to present his particular perspective about who Jesus was, or rather, what being Son of God meant in Mark's eyes. Mark was not thinking in terms of the divinity/humanity question which would preoccupy a later generation; he was not attempting to solve the technical issue of how two natures coexisted in one person. For Mark, Jesus had proclaimed the good news of the kingdom, and Mark realized that this good news was forever inseparable from the person whose story he wanted to record.

Every so often, however, modern readers might find themselves a little bewildered, even put off, by the way Mark has told a portion of his story, with the result that one comes away from the gospel text wondering what sort of impression the disciples were forming of Jesus. In particular, two peculiar stories or tales come to mind: the episode about the demon-possessed Gerasene man (Mk 5:1–20) and the story about the young demon-possessed boy whom the disciples of Jesus were unable to assist (Mk 9:14–29). Each story contains elements of humor as well as of human misery. They read more like tales or legends than like the customary miracle accounts, for in drawing them Mark brushed them with a great deal of color in order to highlight the specialness of Jesus, who can occasion fear, amazement and awe in people.

An Unlikely Messenger

Given its cultural disgust for unclean animals like pigs, a Jewish audience would have found the story about the demons who rushed into the herd of swine and subsequently perished in the lake to be very amusing. And not just one or two animals perished, but a herd about two thousand strong! The imagination needs to supply the sounds of the squealing herd and their frenzied ranting and raving as the demons drove them crazy and caused them to stampede down the steep hillside. The wretched man had likewise been driven insane by the multitude of demons who had taken up residence inside his poor body. As Mark recounts the tale, on encountering the demon-possessed man, Jesus had begun addressing the unclean spirits and ordering them to leave. At one point, the demons and Jesus are even in conversation, as Jesus questions them about their name. Finally, they submit to the command of Jesus, having first secured the curious permission to take up residence in the herd; but unclean as they are, even the pigs do not want them.

Needless to say, the herd's owners were not at all pleased, and the townsfolk, for whom this must have been a first encounter with Jesus, were "seized with fear" as they saw the madman of the hillside in his right mind and two thousand pigs floating belly-up in the lake. They implore Jesus to go away, while the man who got his self-possession back begs Jesus to let him accompany him. Instead, Jesus commissions him to be a kind of apostle among the Gentiles: "Go home to your family and announce to them all that the Lord in his pity has done for you" (Mk 5:19). He departs in order to announce far and wide the great mercy and grace which he had been shown. His enthusiastic witness will prepare the way for the eventual arrival of the early Christian missionaries. The fact that Jesus refers to himself here as "Lord" suggests that the event (if there ever really was such an episode) has been polished as a result of Easter faith.

Apart from the story's fantastic elements, we have basically a scene involving someone (in this case a Gentile and thus, from a biblical perspective, a pagan) who is marginalized in the extreme. He lived among the tombs and there was no way of restraining him; he was the wild, naked man of the Gerasenes. One can well imagine the frightening tales people must have manufactured about him. Jesus and his disciples come upon him, apparently, by accident. What is moving about this encounter is the way Jesus spends time with him: at the beginning he is trying to get the unclean spirits to leave, and at the end he is sitting with the man, who now has both his mind and his clothes.

It is important not to let our imaginations picture Jesus as shouting at the man, as if in angry confrontation with the powers of evil. Jesus appears to be trying to speak with him, and the man, like a frightened animal, is unsure how to react. When was the last time that anyone approached him with respect? When was the last time that anyone recognized in that shredded humanity the image of God? A refreshing calm suddenly descends upon the hillside. This man, who terrified so many people and who had become the legend of the countryside, is mercifully returned to wholeness by someone who treated him, we ought to suppose, like a brother. Not only that, the man did not belong to the people of Israel. Jesus' instruction, "Go home to your family and announce to them all that the Lord in his pity has done for you," thus becomes all the more remarkable. The good news about Jesus, and therefore about the kingdom of God, is going to find its way to the many families and neighborhoods outside of Israel. And, given the circumstances, it is clear that once again God has chosen the most improbable of vehicles to spread that news. Who would have thought that a man whose body housed so many demons that even two thousand swine could not stand them could become a messenger or forerunner of the kingdom of God?

A Father's Faith Restored

The second tale also contains its dramatic features. The disciples of Jesus, sort of like sorcerer's apprentices, have been unable to expel an unclean spirit. In fact, there is a fierce argument going on between the disciples and the scribes, an exchange probably made all the hotter by the disciples' embarrassment and humiliation at not being able to do what their master could do. The boy's father is among the crowd. When Jesus asks about the reason for the argument, the man (whom Mark initially describes merely as "someone from the crowd") speaks out, "Teacher, I have brought to you my son. . . ."

In the sad history that follows, one quickly recognizes the classical symptoms of an epileptic seizure. The people of Jesus' day, as did Jesus himself, had no other way of accounting for such fearful behavior except in terms of demonic possession. As in the previous episode, Jesus then starts to speak with the man. Jesus' question, which we need to imagine being spoken with the utmost compassion, invites the father to share his story with Jesus: "How long has this been happening to him?" And the man begins. Without warning, a "spirit" would seize his son, explains the father, and nearly kill him; to make matters worse, the boy appears to be deaf (and thus speechless) as well.

Once again, one has to picture the various scenes: the frantic father rescuing his son who is just about to fall into a well, or drown in a tub of water, or whose clothes have just caught fire because the seizure has struck the boy while he is playing, close to a kitchen flame or an oil lamp. The defenseless boy cannot even shout out his distress. Such has been the sad story, ever since his son's childhood. How many times had the son almost killed himself? How many times had the parents cried to God, or tried to fathom what they had done to merit such punishment? Perhaps they, like many other distraught parents, had begged God to afflict them and spare their son. It is important to sense the deep, tragic sorrow, bordering on despair, in the father's desperate request, "If you can do anything, have compassion on us and help us" (Mk 9:22). Jesus' response "If you can!" is not a reprimand for lack of faith, but a plea not to give up. Then, with a voice that wants to reassure the man that nothing is impossible with God, Jesus speaks from the depth of his own belief: "Everything is possible to one who has faith." The poor father is nearly beside himself with anguish. How much he must have wanted to believe! How often he must have cried out to God to save his son! And now Jesus, the prophet from Galilee, is telling him after he has wrestled so long that everything is possible to one who truly believes in God. "I do believe," the father cries, in an effort to keep his already stretched faith from shattering. "Help my unbelief!"

And this is where the story should end. The rest of it is anti-climactic. We know that it is going to have a happy ending, because that is the way of most stories. Yet the healing of the boy is not the heart of the story; Mark even omits to tell us about the final reaction of the crowd. The reason the disciples were unable to help, Jesus implies, is that they have not been men of prayer. What was at stake here was not power over demons but an understanding of the struggle of faith. The heart of the story is the father's trial and his struggle to remain a believer when his experience was giving him an altogether different message about God. The way Jesus engaged the man suggests that the father needed healing as much as the son. The greater miracle, then, is that the father has been restored to faith. And this happened, not because of his contact with Jesus' power, but because of his contact with Jesus' own belief. The episode has been mis-titled. It should be "The Restoration of a Father's Faith."

The real power of Jesus, then, lies not in his ability to work miracles but in his ability to help other men and women remain centered on God. Ultimately, it had to be the magnetism of Jesus' faith that drew people to believe that the kingdom of God was near. The disciples of Jesus typically have had another difficult time comprehending the lesson about faith (and thus about the kingdom of God) behind all of Jesus' actions.

PART THREE: WHO IS JESUS?

18

A Matter of Identity

So they asked him, "What are you then? Are you Elijah?" And he said, "I am not." "Are you the Prophet?" He answered, "No." So they said to him, "Who are you, so we can give an answer to those who sent us? What do you have to say for yourself?" (Jn 1:21–22)

One of the curious incidents in Mark's story is the calming of the stormy sea in chapter four. The strange feature of this episode is that Jesus remained sound asleep, on a cushion, while a violent squall threatened to sink the boat. The attentive reader is quick to realize that the story would become doubly curious if Jesus were merely pretending to sleep, in order to test his disciples' faith. That sort of behavior on Jesus' part would be manipulative and unfair. Nor would the suggestion that Jesus had fallen into a very deep slumber solve anything. The believability of the story would be undone by the proposal that anyone could sleep undisturbed by the crashing of wind and waves, and the frantic screams of the disciples. Of course, some readers would take great comfort in the fact that Jesus could do such things as walk on water, or calm the winds. They tend to allegorize the text. Just as Jesus calmed the stormy sea, he can also calm the storms in our lives. So long as Jesus is "in the boat" with us, we are safe. But I would wager that the story was not about something which had actually taken place; rather, it depicted one way by which believers later came to express their faith in Jesus. The question asked by the disciples is, "Who is this whom even wind and sea obey?" (4:41) But the logic of the question is really affirmative: Jesus is the one to whom even the winds and the seas listen.

Now, it would be difficult to ascertain under what sort of circumstances such a faith affirmation emerged, unless as an experience of a miraculous deliverance by the risen Jesus from some impending disaster. If Jesus had actually brought calm to the wind and waves, if he had actually walked on water, then it becomes extremely hard to understand why he could not have used some of his superhuman powers to avoid being killed. And if one were to reply that Jesus voluntarily suspended those powers, then the passion story would be reduced to a charade. Besides, the Jesus of the passion account, and of many other scenes in the gospel narrative, is not the superhuman Jesus who walks upon the waters. That is why the reader's suspicions are aroused when the figure of Jesus becomes too large for ordinary mortals to relate to. The way the early communities related to the risen Jesus was quite different from the way the disciples related to him while he walked among them.

In terms of the narrative, the question, "Who then is this whom even wind and sea obey?" forces the reader to pause and wonder. It is for our benefit, rather than for the benefit of the disciples, that the question is asked. Indeed, there may well have been an occasion when the disciples and Jesus were almost swamped by the waters of the lake, and one might even imagine Jesus (who had not been reared near the water) getting fiercely sick as the boat tossed and turned. He would have been utterly useless in assisting his friends to regain control of the boat. And yet, the boat never capsized: whether it happened by luck or by providential design, at the time the disciples must have been immensely relieved and grateful. Only later, in light of the truth which Easter unveiled, would they have begun to remember in a different light what had happened that evening on the lake. The question about Jesus' identity in this scene ("Who is this?") is post-resurrectional; it is intended to give the reader (or listener) an opportunity to declare his or her faith in the risen Jesus. Otherwise, the fantastic elements of the story are going to alienate historically-minded people.

Mark's Question to the Reader

But the text which normally serves as the point of departure for reflecting on the identity of Jesus is Jesus' question to Peter, "But who do you say that I am?" (Mk 8:29). The disciples and Jesus had been walking toward the villages of Caesarea Philippi, and something prompted Jesus to ask, "Who do people say that I am?" (8:27) People clearly took Jesus to be a prophet, because the disciples answered, "John the Baptist, others Elijah, still others one of the prophets" (8:28). This does not seem to satisfy Jesus, however; hence, his question to Peter. And Peter reassures Jesus that, as far as he and his companions are concerned, Jesus is the Messiah. The disciples had yet to learn, however, that God's Messiah would have to suffer. Three predictions follow in which Jesus discloses to the disciples what fate awaits him in Jerusalem. Even so, the disciples fail to catch the point. Again, this slowness on the part of the disciples arouses our suspicion. While Jesus must have had a growing sense of what lay in the future for him, he probably did not foresee his future in detail. If he had been so clear about his approaching passion and death, then his disciples ought to have been better prepared; and if Jesus had actually predicted his being raised on the third day, then one would think that at least a few of the disciples would have posted themselves by the tomb of Jesus in order to witness such a stupendous marvel.

The fact that Jesus reveals the future to his disciples privately may, at least as far as Mark is concerned, account for why the crowds, not to mention Jesus' enemies, did not station themselves by the tomb, too. Perhaps, therefore, the three predictions of Jesus' suffering and death, and ultimate victory, are strategically placed in the gospel narrative for the sake of the reader. The reader has to be prepared for the startling events of the final week of Jesus' life. Otherwise, the torturing and execution of Jesus would present a grave stumbling block to one who had been told that Jesus was God's Anointed. All of Israel longed for the coming of the Messiah to liberate them, but a Messiah who suffers and dies was not what they had in mind. Furthermore, the resurrection of Jesus would have created an enormous puzzle with respect to God's liberating action on behalf of human beings in this world. What signal would it have given?

We are never told why Jesus raised the question about who people thought he was. Had he suddenly been seized by a crisis of identity? Did he have misgivings about the way people in the villages and towns of Galilee were perceiving him? Had he overheard a conversation among the disciples about rumors they had been picking up as they traveled? Why was this question so important? It must have been a critical question for Mark, because he inserts it at just about the story's midpoint; from this point forward the passion and death of Jesus become pronounced. But it is hard to conceive of Jesus being preoccupied by what people were saying about him. From the perspective of the storyteller, Jesus' question indirectly addresses the reader at this juncture, calling upon the reader (or the hearer) to reach some preliminary judgment about whether he or she wants to remain with Jesus. Peter's affirmation then becomes the reader's own declaration, minus, of course, Peter's misunderstanding (8:32–33).

Of course, it is also quite likely that if the episode had actually occurred, Jesus' reaction to the disciples could have been one of great amusement. "John the Baptist!" Jesus might have humorously exclaimed. "John was beheaded! A prophet of old returned from the grave? What sort of nonsense will people think of next?" It would have made greater sense if people had said that Jesus was *like* John, or *like* Elijah, or *like* one of Israel's classical prophets. Thus, dismissing the rumors and silliness of the crowds, he could have gone on to ask the disciples what *they* thought, assuming their heads were screwed on a little more tightly. Peter's answer is serious, however, and Jesus' subsequent correction of Peter is even more serious.

Again, if this scene actually did take place, I would argue that the difficulty here was not so much contrasting definitions or expectations of messiahship, but rather quite different ways of thinking about God: "You are not thinking as God does, but as human beings do" (8:33). Peter should not be blamed for holding onto a more politically toned notion of messiah (most people did), but he could be faulted for not thinking with the mind of the kingdom of God wherein the values of the present age are reversed. The scene throws us back to the episode of Jesus' temptation in the wilderness as Matthew and Luke imagined it: "Get away, Satan!" (Mt 4:10), for scripture says, "You shall not put the Lord, your God, to the test" (Lk 4:12). Could it be that Jesus had already wrestled with the prospect that if he allowed himself to be martyred the way John the Baptist was, God might be dared into rescuing him? Had Jesus finally come to terms with the idea that, if his commitment to proclaiming the kingdom of God eventuated in his death, he would not thereby have been tempting God to protect him, lest he dash his foot against a stone? The vehemence of Jesus' rebuke to

Peter only makes sense if it reflects a great struggle in Jesus' own soul about what course to take. Peter, in other words, had challenged Jesus' painful discernment.

Jesus' warning his disciples not to tell anyone about his being the Messiah is a primary example of the so-called "secrecy theme" in Mark's story; in terms of the story, it helps to explain why the people of Jesus' day did not acknowledge him as God's Anointed. They did not acknowledge him because Jesus had kept his true identity a secret, although it remains a mystery why Jesus would have done so historically. Mark may have had reasons to keep Jesus' identity a secret until the moment when, at the cross, the Roman centurion calls him the Son of God (15:39); but what reasons would Jesus have had? For Jesus, there was no secret identity; there was only the kingdom of God, and there was his trusted experience that God loved him as a son.

Who One Thinks Jesus Is Depends Upon How One Views What He Has Been Doing

The identity question, then, is framed around a prediction of Jesus' approaching death. He would be killed, not out of some cosmic necessity that decreed the death of the innocent one as expiation for sin, but because he had offended too many people and was considered a threat to their vested political, economic and religious interests. The crowds regarded him as a prophet because he behaved like a prophet. Who Jesus was, consequently, is a function of what he had been doing to earn himself the title "prophet." By the same token, Mark's central claim is that Jesus is the Son of God, a title which needs to be very carefully understood. Thus, Jesus is portrayed as the one who is faithful to God. He listens to God; he preaches, heals and forgives sins; he shares the peculiar divine affection for the defenseless, the poor, and the outcast; he makes a conscious decision to become poor himself, in order to live in solidarity with those at the bottom of the social ladder; he speaks boldly, bearing witness to the truth honestly and courageously. As a consequence of the way he lived, he is betrayed, humiliated, tortured and put to death. Once again, the meaning of the title "Son of God" is best measured in terms of what Jesus did, how he lived and died, what he stood for.

We Define Who Jesus Is By the Way That We Live

Just as who Jesus was could not be separated from the way he lived, so too who the disciples were cannot be divorced from the way they lived. When Jesus asks them, therefore, "Who do you say that I am?", another way of hearing this question might be, "What are you prepared to do as a result of your being with me?" Or, "How has your being with me changed your life? What are you willing to do now that you would not have done before you met me?"

For us, however, the question of Jesus' identity is not framed in terms of the religious and political imagery of ancient Israel. We cannot simply answer Jesus, "You are the Messiah," the way Peter did in the story (although in some way Peter had actually been answering the question "Who do you say that I am?" since the day he first met Jesus, with or without the title "Messiah," and he would one day answer it with his life). The title Peter assigned to Jesus has even less significance for us than the title "King." The only way for us to respond to Jesus' question is through the way that we live. Thus the answer is not a speculative one; it does not consist of a title or an abstract definition. It is practical or functional: the believer answers Jesus' question, day by day, through the practice of discipleship.

The very same point (which liberation theologians have been making repeatedly) can be found in the text, "Not everyone who says to me, 'Lord, Lord,' will enter the kingdom of heaven, but only the one who does the will of my Father in heaven" (Mt 7:21). In fact, even a person who works miracles, casts out demons and prophesies in Jesus' name, will be denied access to the kingdom, if he or she has failed to do God's will. God's will apparently has little to do with the ability to heal, exorcise demons and utter prophecies.

The most striking illustration of this idea occurs in the final judgment scene of Matthew 25. There individuals are denied entry into God's kingdom because they failed to do elementary services for their own brothers and sisters. The frightening thing is not that Jesus' followers failed to do things for people who were complete strangers to them, but that, as John Donahue explains in The Gospel as Parable (pp. 109–125), they omitted doing things for members of the very same community! It may be true that Jesus expected his disciples to serve, in addition, even those who did not belong to the community, that is to say, the countless men and women whom we encounter over the course of our lives who really have no claim upon our attention apart from the fact that they are human beings in need. But the actions of the unrighteous become all the more reprehensible, and the severity of the divine judgment all the more understandable, when one realizes what is going on. Men and women of the very same community, of the same household of faith, have failed to recognize Jesus (the one who, as Christians, they professed was at the center of their lives) in their brothers and sisters.

Perhaps the major reason why the question about the identity of Jesus needs to be framed in practical rather than abstract or theoretical terms is that many Catholics could not care less, really, about who the church, or the evangelists, or even Jesus himself, claimed that he is. Most of the titles traditionally conferred upon Jesus, such as Lord, Messiah, Savior, Son of David, Good Shepherd, or Son of God, contain little meaning for them, since these titles arose in a culture and religious ambience far removed from ours. They will use these titles, for lack of more suitable alternatives, and they are both earnest and loyal enough to want to have someone explain to them what the titles actually intended to signify. The basic issue here, however, is not one of Christian literacy. It is an issue of experience. Experientially, titles have to mean as much to us as, for instance, the title "Messiah" denoted for the early disciples. This requires that Jesus first has to be an integral part of our experience, just as he was for Peter and the others. The Messiah, or Anointed of God, would deliver the people of Israel, not only from their sins and transgressions, but also from whatever tyrannies had robbed them of their dignity and freedom as God's chosen people.

So too for us. Jesus needs to be more than a supremely wise moral teacher; we have the philosophers for that. Jesus needs to be more than the world-transcending contemplative who instructs human beings about the righteous path through which they overcome suffering. We have the Buddha for that. Jesus even needs to be more than the prophet who denounces injustice, preaches repentance and recalls men and women to the way of God; we have the voices of Isaiah, Amos, Jeremiah—even John the Baptist—for that. Jesus is the beloved Son through whom God brings the reign of justice into the world; he is the one who makes possible a very new experience of God. Jesus is the one through whom God speaks good news to the poor and liberty to captives.

What, therefore, are we looking for? Moral guidance? Contemplative tranquility? Social critique? Personal deliverance from sin and guilt? Peace of mind? Or does someone have to open our minds and imaginations to embrace a very different possibility for the world, even another way of being human together? And once opened to that possibility, who will help us to realize it?

19

Being Son

Whatever interest Mark has in Jesus' identity is locked up with the title Son of God. The proclamation that Jesus is God's Son opens the narrative (Mk 1:1), and Jesus' relationship with God as his Father recurs at key moments: the baptism (1:11), the transfiguration (9:7), the agony in the garden (14:36), and the crucifixion (15:39). In 14:61 the high priest demands that Jesus tell him whether or not he is "the Messiah, the son of the Blessed One" (a question which would have been senseless unless Jesus had given some public indication of a special relationship with God). In 12:1–12 Jesus delivers a parable about some wicked tenants who wind up seizing and assassinating a landowner's "beloved son," a parable with clear allegorical reference to Jesus and the faithless religious leaders of Israel. Following each of the passion predictions, Mark includes lessons about self-denial (8:34–35), service (9:35–37) and not ambitioning seats of privilege and power over one's brothers and sisters (10:42–45). Each of these three texts provides further insight into what being son means for Mark. The categories Mark employs for defining divinity are obedience, which takes the form of radical listening and radical openness, always conscious and free, to the mystery of God in one's life; powerlessness, service, and poverty. The Jesus who counseled a rich man to sell what he owned and give the proceeds to the poor must have adopted the same manner of living himself. Throughout the gospel, Mark presents Jesus preferring the humbler designation "Son of man," and this Jesus absolutely declines being called good, since God alone is good (10:18). Nor does he know all that God knows (13:32).

Once again, it may be worth recalling that Mark's faith has colored the way he retold the story of Jesus. Throughout the narrative, the reader is constantly being engaged by Mark's faith, a fact which is both understandable and unavoidable. If the reactions of students I have taught can be generalized, I would say that modern readers run into trouble precisely at those points where Mark's faith has been shaped or conditioned by circumstances which are foreign to us. For example, while we can readily relate to the experience of being in the thick of controversy, we may find it puzzling that people quarreled with Jesus over healing someone, or plucking grain, on the sabbath: was the religious issue all that serious? Or again, it is well known that because Mark was writing for a Christian community facing the threat of persecution, his gospel features the cross in Jesus' life and the suffering entailed in the practice of discipleship. The same prospect has been a constant menace to many communities in Central and South America today, but it does not apply to those of us in North America. Thus, our religious tastes might gravitate more towards the gospels of Luke and Matthew, who wrote under a different, more stable set of circumstances. Many of Jesus' disputes with religious leaders appear to reflect situations encountered by the early communities rather than historical episodes from Jesus' life. Just as Mark's Jesus was historically detached from the circumstances of Jesus' own day, so too we are quite removed historically from the situation of Mark's day. In short, what being son meant for Mark might well have been somewhat different for Jesus.

Jesus' Call Also Had Its History

There must have been various pressures, therefore, which worked upon Mark so that in composing his version of the story he stressed the categories of service, poverty and powerlessness. But just as Mark's portrait of Jesus was shaped by concerns and circumstances which today can be pieced together through some very careful biblical detective work, so too Jesus' own experience of God was affected by the situation and circumstances which he faced. However sudden and dramatic the divine revelation he heard at the moment of his baptism, Jesus would not have been able to hear anything unless he had been predisposed, even prepared, to recognize God's voice. God's voice would have had to be contextualized within Jesus' own experience in order for him to respond. That voice would have had its "pre-history" in the silent days at Nazareth, Jesus' so-called "hidden years." It would have been there that Jesus reflected, prayed, learned about himself, people and human nature, and divined something about Israel's hopes and Israel's God. There, amidst those silent years, the world would have shown itself as essentially a welcoming place where life was indeed "gracious." There the profound truths of the Old Testament seeped into Jesus' soul, and there any news about the momentous events of the day trickled into village life. It would have been there that Jesus' own social and political outlook took shape, and that his human qualities matured as he interacted with his family and the people of his village. There, too, the imagination of Jesus developed its patterns. First and foremost, then, being son required his being fully human.

Clearly, then, the heavenly voice did not create Jesus to be son at the moment of his baptism. The words "with you I am well pleased" seem to indicate that God had been pleased with Jesus for quite some time. When, we might ask, did the disciples become aware of God's having been well pleased with Jesus? Could Jesus have shared this intimate experience with them? If these words were addressed to Jesus at his baptism, would it have been all that important for the disciples to know about them soon afterwards? Or is the approval we are hearing in these words, which is repeated at the scene of the transfiguration, actually the Father's approval of the *crucified* Jesus? For the fact of the matter is that they really would assume the most profound significance as the words accompanying the divine action of raising Jesus from the dead. By recounting these words at the moment of Jesus' baptism, Mark has identified Jesus for the reader: the one with whom God is well pleased is the one whom God has raised from the dead, and this is precisely what being son means in the fullest sense. The resurrection, in other words, authenticated God's being well pleased with Jesus. It is this authentication which Mark has obviously extended backwards to the scene of the baptism, and which, of course, could be extended back even further.

The One Whom God Loved

On this showing, the reason that God was well pleased with Jesus has to do with his life and death, that is, his being radically open to the voice of God, even to death upon the cross. But we could add to this. God could have been pleased with Jesus' integrity and his readiness to devote himself to the cause of the kingdom of God, just as the other prophets did. God could have been pleased that Jesus trusted the divine promise to liberate the people of Israel, and all the nations of the world, from sin and oppression. God could have been pleased because Jesus' heart and mind mirrored God's own concerns, because Jesus fully and brilliantly reflected the divine image and likeness. Jesus was Son of God because he behaved like a son of God, and he behaved like a son because God had communicated himself to Jesus as Father, in a way both absolutely mysterious and practically beyond words. The only language which adequately conveys what Jesus' being son or child of God means is the resurrection itself.

The word "Son" (or the experience behind it) had not fallen on deaf ears. In some way, the heavenly voice had to be as much confirmation as revelation. It is this fact which enabled the other gospel writers to push the notion of sonship back further into Jesus' early life. But we must not allow their rendering of Jesus' sonship or their theologizing of his origins to distract us from the more important and more basic point that being son was something which Jesus experienced.

Humiliation, suffering and death belonged to the cross, which indelibly imprinted itself from the very beginning upon the church's memory, imagination and understanding. How could things have developed otherwise, given what had taken place in Jerusalem that final week? Yet the fact is that the cross probably did not shape the memory, imagination and understanding of Jesus himself. Whatever effect it had upon him would come toward the very end, and it would have been intimately connected with Jesus' unconquerable trust in God's power to bring about the kingdom. There was no mystique of suffering in the teaching of Jesus, no spiritual advice on how to cope with it, no theological justification for it in terms of the practice of asceticism. While the cross figures constitutively into Mark's understanding of Jesus as God's Son, and while the same was true for Paul, the same cannot be said of Jesus. The foreboding which hovers over the gospel story because of our knowledge of its outcome on Calvary hardly needs to have been present throughout Jesus' life. If that had been the case, then the extraordinary joy of the initial proclamation about God's good news would have been terribly unfounded, and Jesus would have been utterly deceived.

Being son would certainly involve obedience, and obedience under the form of faithfulness to his experience of God and his vision of the kingdom would eventually lead Jesus to his death. But the cross alone would not define sonship. Jesus had been seized by the divine promise. Joyously and enthusiastically he spoke about God: a God who liberates, a God who throws banquets, a God whose love is as reckless as it is unlimited, a God who detests anything and everything which defaces human beings, a God who can be trusted as a father, a God with whom men and women can be on the most intimate terms, a God who forgives. Indeed, the one thread which pulls the gospels together most consistently is Jesus' assuring human beings of divine forgiveness.

The themes of suffering and sacrifice as major motifs in the church's understanding of Jesus would become quite pronounced as time went on. The letter to the Hebrews states: "Son though he was, he learned obedience from what he suffered" (Heb 5:8). Jesus' death on the cross would be viewed as expiation for human sins. Yet while the forgiveness of sins and the cross are certainly connected, the connection is not quite so direct as various New Testament texts would suggest. Jesus began reassuring men and women of God's mercy and forgiveness, long before the cross started coming into view. The link between the cross and forgiveness, which got submerged somewhere, was God's promise to set human beings free. On this point the Latin American theologians are absolutely correct. The good news which Jesus proclaimed at the beginning was liberation and freedom, a theme more fully spelled out in Luke. Being forgiven came under the broader notion of being set free, for there were other things from which human beings needed to be liberated besides their sin and guilt. If one prefers to regard the power of sin as the full range of evils which keep men and women poor, oppressed and dehumanized, then one is bringing the hidden link to surface. The cross thereby becomes the great symbol of the desire and the price of our liberation or redemption. The cross should never be allowed to eclipse the good news which Jesus first announced; the cross must confirm it. While the cross in itself is not good news (for, like any sign, the cross needs to be interpreted or put in a context), the revelation of God's love as the ultimate (and invincible) liberating power in the world is absolutely wonderful. It is the promise of God, conceived as the divine promise to liberate, which ties the Old and New Testaments together, and not the forgiveness of sins as such. Forgiveness, after all, was not new with Jesus, as anyone familiar with the prophets or the Psalms realizes.

20

Jesus' Experience of God

"No one knows who the Son is except the Father, and who the Father is except the Son and anyone to whom the Son wishes to reveal him" (Lk 10:22).

This may seem like a puzzling text with which to begin thinking about Jesus' experience of God; the sentiment it expresses sounds too high to be coming from the lips of the down-to-earth Jesus whose story we have been tracing. This verse serves the purpose, however, of showing the connection between Jesus' faith and ours, or between his experience of God and our own. The faith of the church traces back through countless generations of believers to the faith of the earliest Christian communities, and the faith of those communities rested upon the faith of Jesus. Upon being asked one time about his religious background, Fr. Karl Rahner, who was arguably the most influential Catholic theologian of the twentieth century, replied that he was Catholic because his parents were. The same could probably be said about nearly every one of us. We inherited our faith from our families, and the first generation of believers inherited their faith from Jesus.

What we are ultimately trusting, therefore, is Jesus' experience of God. In any question about becoming or remaining Christian, what is basically at stake is the credibility of Jesus. And somehow the word "Father" has come to abbreviate the whole range of Jesus' experience of God. It is unlikely that the above text from Luke came from the lips of Jesus, since it reflects a later stage of the community's faith development. But the text accurately reflects the church's dependence upon Jesus for its experience of God. This was not a causal dependence, either, but a conditional one. The early communities did not know

God because of Jesus, as if Jesus were a source of new and definitive information about God; they knew God in and through Jesus. That is, their experience and knowledge of God was always contingent upon their being with Jesus, the "Son" who makes the "Father" known.

These comments might help to bring out the relevance of the question about Jesus' experience of God. The fact is that virtually everything Jesus did and said arose out of that experience. That experience was the source of Jesus' freedom and his openness; it colored his refreshing acceptance of the everyday world. It is what distinguished him from John the Baptist, Elijah and the great prophets of Israel's past. It was on the basis of his experience (which he trusted) that he could say to Peter in the matter of forgiving his brother, for example, "I say to you, not seven times but seventy-seven times" (Mt 18:22). How did Jesus know this? Why was he so certain that God would behave this way toward each of us? Because this is what his experience was telling him.

The reality of this connection between Jesus' faith and ours is confirmed in the letter to the Romans, where Paul writes:

> For you did not receive a spirit of slavery to fall back into fear, but you received a spirit of adoption, through which we cry, *Abba,* "Father!" The Spirit itself bears witness with our spirit that we are children of God (Rom 8:15–16).

In other words, the brother or sister of Jesus has no reason ever to be afraid of or run away from God, the way Adam was afraid when he and Eve hid themselves from God in the garden (Gen 3:10). The very same Spirit which made Jesus God's Son makes us daughters and sons of God, too. But this relationship, which describes the ultimate truth about us, is only fully realized and appreciated through faith; this relationship is also experiential. One experiences oneself to be a son or daughter of God, that is, as loved, raised and cared for by the Father himself.

Jesus Knew God, As a Person of Faith

What else could have been the source of Jesus' confidence, except his experience of God? When Mark reports that Jesus could work no miracles in Nazareth because the people there lacked faith (Mk 6:5–6), or when Jesus told the pleading father of an epileptic boy, "Everything is possible to one who has faith" (Mk 9:23), or when he said to the woman with a hemorrhage, "Daughter, your faith has saved you" (Mk 5:34), we have to suppose that he was speaking out of his experience. At this early stage of the tradition, Jesus was not the object of faith; God was. Jesus had no privileged access to the mystery of God which by-passed all that is involved in being a believer. Miracles happened because *Jesus himself believed in their possibility.*

And how could Jesus be so sure that God was a God who would heal? How could he be so sure that mercy counted more than sacrifice? Because such was his experience of God. Jesus would have been un-able to teach or to preach what he did not believe himself. He was able to tell his followers that they must love their enemies, because he knew that God had no enemies, any more than God differentiated between Samaritans and Jews, or between the clean and the unclean. God beheld all men and women as daughters and sons, which made all of us brothers and sisters. Nearly everything in the gospel can be boiled down to the way God was, the God of Jesus' experience. And what Christians apprehend in their experience is God-in-Jesus.

The First Parable: A Reflection of Jesus' Faith

Let us consider as an example the parable of the sower in Mark 4:1–9. Mark must have considered this parable important, because it is the lead parable of his gospel, and both Matthew and Luke followed suit. By setting this parable prominently at the early stages of Jesus' ministry, Mark appears to be suggesting that it is a key or a frame for evaluating the success of Jesus' mission. If Jesus began his public life as enthusiastically as the story suggests, then we could imagine him, once the initial excitement of the crowds began to wear off, wondering where his efforts were leading. Maybe he found himself sitting one morning in the shade near a field where a farmer was sowing. He watches, distractedly, until suddenly he associates the action of the farmer with what he himself had been doing travelling among the villages of Galilee, preaching and teaching. Some seed falls on the narrow path between the fields, some falls on rocky ground, some falls among briars: some is eaten by birds, some is choked by weeds, and some is scorched by the sun. That pretty much sums up the reactions of the crowds, too! And yet the parable also reveals Jesus' enormous hope in God's power to work marvels among those who respond to the word: "And some seed fell on rich soil and produced fruit. It came up and grew and yielded thirty, sixty, and a hundredfold" (Mk 4:8). Such a harvest would have been inconceivable to the ordinary farmer; as Jesus recounts the parable, it sounds as if his own charismatic enthusiasm and confidence rushed through with the story's surprising end.

The parable sheds light on Jesus' experience precisely because it originates in his imagination as an attempt to come to terms with what had been happening in his life. Furthermore, the early communities must have sensed this. By preserving the parable, they allowed it to light up their experience, too. What this and other kingdom parables do is to nuance the gospel's message about the kingdom or reign of God. The kingdom is not the brilliant, show-stopping spectacle of dramatic power and victory, but a much humbler reality. Jesus' own expectations about the kingdom, as well as his vision of what the kingdom might be, must have been constantly modified by his experience. He had to have been learning a great deal about the ways of God, just as every person of faith who is truly open to the divine mystery must.

The Kingdom, Not the Cross, Was the Center of Jesus' Mission

Because of the way the gospel was composed, the overall gospel narrative appears split into two parts, intimating that Jesus came preaching the kingdom, encountered rejection, and as a result of being rejected turned his attention to Jerusalem and the cross. The cross was not a backup justification for his mission, however. The logic of the story demands that Jesus himself had to be in the process of development and continually learning through a prayerful reflection upon his experience. His mission was shaped by all sorts of circumstances, encounters and events; his vision was tested and tempered by history.

In general, the human response to God's desire to liberate has been neither positive nor uniform. Liberation sounds wonderful, but there is a cost: human hearts have to change if the human world is going to become liberated from the power of sin, especially sin under the form of injustice. Concretely, that requires, for example, some sort of revolution. Rulers will have to be thrown down from their thrones, the rich sent away empty-handed, the proud scattered in their conceit, while the poor and the powerless will be lifted up, and the hungry will be filled with the choicest of foods (Lk 1:51–53). These are radical sentiments indeed, coming as they do, in Luke's gospel, from the lips of Jesus' mother!

The resistances to Jesus' preaching, the unevenness of human response, and the apparently meager results illustrate why those who dedicate themselves to the work of human liberation pay a price. The point needs to be repeated: the cross does not appear in Jesus' life as the validation of his work. It does not confer meaning upon his call and his mission by becoming some kind of transcendental sign, transforming Jesus into a cosmic symbol of humanity's being redeemed. The cross alone fails to rescue Jesus' mission, which was to bring good news to the poor (Lk 4:18), from collapse. No, the history of the sower has to be taken seriously: some seed is going to fall by the wayside. The cross is the consequence of Jesus' commitment to the kingdom of God and the work of liberation which would usher it in. Whatever theological meaning it might assume for Christians will come later, as the church contemplated the whole Jesus story, from start to finish, in terms of the divine creative plan to endow men and women with the freedom of the children of God. In the end, Jesus profoundly believed, the harvest would be extraordinary; but first we would have to learn how to discern the kingdom's presence, since, oddly enough, its features and form may be so humble and ordinary that we could pass right over it.

Jesus Acted as One Who Had Divine Approval

From time to time, people inquire about what Jesus might have been aware of in terms of his self-understanding. He undoubtedly viewed himself as someone in the prophetic tradition especially charged with announcing the kingdom of God. Inwardly, Jesus would have possessed an unbreakable sense of having been sent. Thus, Jesus' experience of God would have been at the root of whatever authority he himself claimed; he knew himself to be the servant or beloved son whom God had chosen to proclaim the kingdom. This would have been the answer to the question thrown at Jesus by the chief priests, the scribes and the elders during the eventful final days in Jerusalem: "By what authority are you doing these things? Or who gave you this authority to do them?" (Mk 11:28) In other words, the authority Jesus claimed was not that of someone born to a high station, or appointed to a powerful position: his authority did not reside in his position, or his origins, or some title, or even in his own person. It resided, rather, in his mission or vocation as servant of the kingdom. It was God himself who warranted or approved what Jesus did, since neither Jesus nor the prophets of old enjoyed authority in their own names.

In his book *Jesus, the Servant-Messiah*, Marinus de Jonge writes:

> Jesus not only announced the Kingdom of God; he inaugurated it. This placed him in a unique relationship to God, and he was aware of it when he addressed God as Father. It is probable that he regarded himself as the Messiah and Son of David inspired and empowered by the Spirit. We do not know whether he called himself Son of God, but he certainly spoke and acted as the Son on whom the Father had bestowed everything to be his servant at a supreme moment: the long-awaited turning point in human history (p. 75).

Whether or not Jesus ever thought of himself as Messiah and Son of David, I am not sure. But what does seem clear is that the source of whatever self-identity Jesus possessed was most likely shaped by his profound intimacy with the God of Israel, whom he knew as Father. The prophet who finally announced the realization of God's long-awaited promise was someone who had experienced God in an arrestingly new way.

We Are Not Servants, but Children

The only reason for inquiring about Jesus' experience of God or about his awareness of himself as God's Son is that Jesus' way of relating to God profoundly affects our access to God as well. To examine the religious experience of Jesus for its own sake frames his relationship to God in terms of his identity rather than his mission. To examine it for our sake creates the possibility of our relating to God just as Jesus did. Although he would never have thought of himself as possessing divine status (Mk 10:18), there is little doubt that he confidently thought of himself as close enough to God to address him intimately as Father. As John Donahue wonderfully explains in *The Gospel as Parable*, in recounting the parable about the runaway son, Luke has effectively captured the revolutionary nature of Jesus' picture of God (Lk 15:11–32). Both the younger and the older son mistakenly believed that the appropriate way to relate to their father was as a servant (15:19) or as a slave (15:29). The father overcome with emotion who ran to embrace his returning son, and who later went outside to plead with his angry elder son to join the feast, has behaved in a very uncharacteristic way. Such compassion, such refusal to stand on his dignity as the patriarchal head of his family, such refusal to allow his sons to regard him as their master, reveals to us that Luke caught the insight about Jesus' experience of God as our Father. Through the parable, Luke has defined what divine fatherhood means. It means redefining sonship: we are no longer slaves, but children (Rom 8:16).

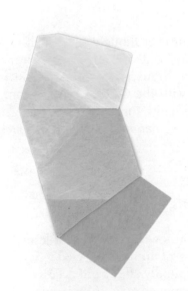

21

Why Did Jesus Have to Be Divine?

The great revelation of God was not actually about the identity of Jesus but about God's readiness to initiate the definitive liberation of the people of Israel and of the world. Jesus revealed that God was about to make good on the divine promise by inaugurating what he referred to as the kingdom of God. Any discussion about the divinity of Jesus has to keep this in view, for everything begins with God's absolutely free, loving determination to create the human race and then to liberate it from every form of oppression. This creating and liberating God stands at the center of the story of Jesus. His faith was thoroughly theocentric, and thus the church's devotional piety with respect to Jesus ought to be oriented theocentrically, too. Too often people's thinking about the divinity of Jesus is encumbered by bothersome presuppositions, which amount to nothing more than guesses as to what being divine is all about. The longer we stay within the gospel story, however, the more those presuppositions gradually undo themselves.

Naturally, the question "Why did Jesus have to be divine?" needs to be raised and addressed in the course of talking about Jesus today, but the question is not fully ripe until one is fairly well immersed in the gospel story. Sometimes the divinity question has been prompted by ideological concerns, particularly among socially and religiously conservative Christians who sense a connection between Jesus' possessing divine status and institutional authority both in the church and in civil society. Any diminishment of Jesus' divinity threatens them, not so much because their belief about Jesus has been challenged but because they perceive that the security of their worlds has been undermined. In these cases, the question is almost always premature.

The early church came to attribute divine status to Jesus more or less as a conclusion, based on what it saw to be the implications of his being raised from the dead. From the pages of the fourth gospel, it is the risen Jesus who speaks out of his definitive oneness with the Father: "The Father and I are one" (Jn 10:30). And Luke wrote in the Acts of the Apostles (Peter is speaking):

> God raised this Jesus; of this we are all witnesses. Exalted at the right hand of God, he received the promise of the holy Spirit from the Father and poured it forth, as you [both] see and hear. . . . Therefore let the whole house of Israel know for certain that God has made him both Lord and Messiah, this Jesus whom you crucified. (Acts 2:32–36)

In his book *Christology in the Making*, James Dunn traced the New Testament origins of the doctrine of the incarnation, that is, the Word of God becoming flesh, which is based on the text of John 1:14. It was the doctrine of the incarnation, rather than the resurrection, which played the major role in the subsequent development of the church's "high" teaching about the divinity of Christ, which was expressed in terms of Jesus' possessing two "natures." Such studies are important, because they address the critical question about whether and at what stage the New Testament ever clearly and unequivocally called Jesus God. Often, those texts which appear to be the clearest and most unambiguous about Jesus' divinity turn out to be far more qualified and temperate than a superficial reading would suggest.

The problem is that the status of Jesus as divine frequently becomes the center of attention in a person's mind before he or she has appropriated the dynamics of discipleship. True, most non-believers would not be drawn to notice Jesus at all unless the church proclaimed him as Lord and God's Son. Since Jesus enjoys such status, the logic runs, he obviously must be important and merits the attention of all God-seeking men and women; therefore, the church's claims about him should be carefully listened to and closely examined. I would argue, however, that the logic of conversion normally runs a little differently. There is something going on in the lives of Jesus' followers and in the communities joined in his name which makes outsiders wonder about the source of the Christian difference. In other words, it is the practice of the gospel which ought to be arousing interest and curiosity on the part of outsiders. The lived demonstration of an immensely attractive way of being human holds enormous persuasive power. Discipleship, or example, is what proves the integrity of faith. For John, this could be summed up as love: "This is how all will know that you are my disciples, if you have love for one another" (Jn 13:35).

The fully-blown expression or articulation of the church's belief in the divinity of Jesus came in the fifth century with the Council of Chalcedon's declaration that Jesus Christ is "true God, true man." Yet what guided the early Christian reflection about Jesus was not so much the issue of identity as it was the issue of salvation. The church of the fourth and fifth centuries had backed into the insight that Jesus would have had to be divine in order to live the way he did and, even more importantly as far as people like us are concerned, we would have to be divine in order to follow him along that way. The category of divinity, therefore, could never be dissociated from history: it could never be allowed to degenerate into an esoteric exploration into the nature of Jesus, as if that nature had no bearing on the way we become fully human and express our humanity. If divinity were attributed to Jesus in such a way that it was his exclusive privilege to be Son of God, then there would be no point in adding to the credal statements the phrases "for us" and "for our salvation." What Jesus was had a direct impact upon our being empowered to live as he did, as the Father expected his daughters and sons to live in this world.

Where the early Christian insight gets cloudy, however, is in its concentration upon a particular humanistic approach to virtue as an expression of being divine. The ascetical and ethical ideals against which the early Christian writers elaborated the practice of discipleship actually had lost touch with the story and traditions about Jesus, especially his passionate dedication to the kingdom of God and to the prophetic work of justice which that implied. Moral perfection became an ideal or a goal in and of itself, detached from the kingdom of God as a concrete, historical reality. The kingdom was theologized, spirited away into a heavenly realm, and perhaps understandably so. Everyone knew that the kingdom as Jesus seemed to have envisioned it failed to arrive. In its place, one now had the church, the pilgrim people of God journeying in history toward its true homeland, which was heaven.

But the failure of Jesus' enthusiastic vision ought not to have drawn people away from history toward heaven. It was unfortunate that no one rethought the kingdom of God's relation to history in a novel way: God's decisive and liberating action could still have been viewed as taking place within history, reshaping it and making it ever more human, even though the end of the world was not imminent. Instead, Christianity became increasingly a powerful world religion, which profoundly affected the course of world history. The lesson of the sower had been forgotten.

Divinization versus Humanization

At any rate, to return to our opening question, it is important to note that, while divinity and divinization (our becoming divine and sharing in the divine nature) were major concerns for the early church, today's concern is humanization, as nearly every reputable contemporary theologian has pointed out in one way or another. As a result, while a great deal of the early theological reflection was devoted to understanding what the divinity of Jesus was all about, the attention of many theologians today has concentrated on his being human. And the purpose is still salvific or redemptive: how are men and women to follow someone whom they do not understand and relate to?

Furthermore, just as the early writers attempted to work through their reflection about the divine nature of Jesus in terms of a doctrine of salvation, and unavoidably adopted the human ascetical and ethical ideals of their day; so also contemporary writers have tried to work through their reflection about the humanness of Jesus in terms of a doctrine of full human integration or liberation, and have understandably been influenced by the social and history-transforming ideas which first came to be explored by Karl Marx. Both then and now, we might say, Christian writers came under the influence of "pagan" authors as they tried to articulate the most profound insights into the nature of Christian practice. Jesus could never be Socrates, any more than he could ever have been an early version of Marx.

Why is the divinity of Jesus of such great concern to the church? Because at stake is the integrity of our humanity, and the ultimate liberation or redemption of human beings and their communities. Only the presence of God among us could finally transform human history from within.

PART FOUR:
THE LAST DAYS

22

What Did Jesus Know, and When Did He Know It?

One of the frequently recurring questions many people raise is about Jesus' foreknowledge. The gospel story seems to imply that Jesus clearly knew the future, and the person who knows the future must in some way be divine. Since Jesus is divine, the argument runs, he must have known far more than he ever let on. In particular, the passion narratives can reenforce this impression, where Jesus is presented as self-assured and in control even as the situation around him is deteriorating. Jesus foresees the room where he and his disciples will eat the Passover meal together, and also predicts the betrayal by Judas and the triple denial by Peter. This merely confirms that everything appears to be unfolding according to the divine plan, which Jesus foresaw and which the prophets had foretold.

One of the things that holds this sort of reasoning in check, however, is Jesus' statement about the coming of the last day: "But of that day or hour, no one knows, neither the angels in heaven, *nor the Son*, but only the Father" (Mk 13:32). The conclusion to be drawn is that Jesus did not know the future the way God does; foreknowledge is not a helpful category for understanding what being Son of God is all about. Surely Jesus would have experienced confusion and doubt as the movement he had started began to disintegrate; he had to be pained as he watched the demoralization of his followers, and their fearful collapse in the garden when they found themselves surrounded by an armed crowd. It is hard to imagine that Jesus foresaw failure as part of the divine plan.

The Passion Predictions

On three separate occasions in the second half of his gospel, Mark narrates that Jesus took his disciples aside in order to teach them about the fate that awaited him in Jerusalem. Since Matthew and Luke are doubtlessly following Mark's lead, it is no wonder that they, too, include the three "passion predictions." Likewise, since they are trailing Mark, it is no wonder that they incorporate the story of Jesus' transfiguration (Mk 9:2–8). This scene serves the purpose in Mark's gospel of providing divine reaffirmation of Jesus' words to his disciples about the meaning and necessity of his approaching suffering and death. Because Jesus' prediction and his teaching about the cross must have been extremely difficult for the disciples to hear, let alone comprehend, the storyteller reintroduces the divine voice which spoke at Jesus' baptism: "This is my beloved Son. Listen to him" (Mk 9:7).

On each of the three occasions, Jesus' prediction about his approaching passion, death and resurrection is accompanied by an instruction which interprets the mystery of the cross, for the cross will be as inevitable for the disciple as it was for Jesus himself:

> "Whoever wishes to come after me must deny himself, take up his cross, and follow me. For whoever wishes to save his life will lose it, but whoever loses his life for my sake and that of the gospel will save it. What profit is there for one to gain the whole world and forfeit his life?" (Mk 8:34–36)

After the second prediction Jesus called the Twelve aside once again and instructed them that the one who wishes to be the greatest must become the servant of all (Mk 9:33–37). This lesson is repeated after the third prediction, where Jesus points to himself as living out this teaching first and foremost:

> "Rather, whoever wishes to be great *among you* [as opposed to among the faithless Gentiles] will be your servant; whoever wishes to be first among you will be the slave of all. For the Son of Man did not come to be served but to serve and to give his life as a ransom for many" (Mk 10:43–45).

The meaning of the cross is couched in terms of service. For Jesus, as well as for his companions, authentic liberation or salvation, which the cross symbolizes, cannot be divorced from the firm determination to avoid aspiring to positions of power and influence which might lead to lording it over others. Not possessing wealth, power and influence, men and women of the kingdom become extremely vulnerable to the hostile forces at work in the world. Yet their dedication to the kingdom is itself a service; it could even cost them their lives. Nevertheless, by means of their commitment, their actions and their example, human beings who might otherwise be lost or destroyed through the power of sin and death will be rescued or "ransomed." The greatest act of service and of love, therefore, is risking one's own security, one's pride, one's career or professional standing, even one's very life, in order to help other men and women become free from whatever oppresses them.

Why Mark Primes His Readers

The three passion predictions, uttered so clearly and precisely, are most likely inserted into the gospel story by the evangelist in order to prepare the reader for the tragic events which are about to unfold. Without such a warning or such clues, the outcome of Jesus' story might well scandalize or scare away the reader whose faith has not yet ripened. Judging from the rest of the story, it appears that the disciples never grasped what Jesus was talking about. Their puzzlement, fear and astonishment over the raising of Jesus from the dead suggests that the disciples were by no means prepared for that occurrence. Mark's persistent explanation, namely, their hardness of heart, finally caves in: the disciples did not understand because the meaning and necessity of Jesus' rejection, betrayal, torture and execution had never been all that clear to them. To a later generation, the very idea of a rejected and suffering Messiah would seem both repulsive and self-contradictory. Somehow, the New Testament authors realized, the fate of Jesus had to be looked at from an angle that would enable people to discover in his suffering and death the secret wisdom, the power and the love of God. At the very least, in narrating the story, Mark had to provide his readers with some divine confirmation of Jesus' destiny; everything had to have been foreseen. The notion of Messiah had to be inverted in order to accommodate the stark reality of the cross and the failure of the king-dom to materialize.

Did Jesus, then, actually forecast his death on three distinct occasions, with such clear and precise detail? Probably not. Did Peter, James and John actually behold Jesus in conversation with Moses and Elijah, and hear the Father's voice thunder approval of Jesus? Again, probably not. In order to appreciate this, we need to shift our mental processes so that we start thinking as a storyteller might. The gospel narrative is not, and was never intended to be, an historical chronicle. Mark's intention was to invent a way of handing on the memories and traditions about Jesus, the Son of God, who had come announcing the arrival of the kingdom, and to explain what being son was all about. In doing so, Mark created the Christian story form we call a gospel. Now, if we ask whether Jesus in the history behind the story ever had any idea about what lay in store for him, the answer has to be yes. And if we inquire further whether he might have tried to help his companions understand why what had happened to the other prophets would also happen to him, once again the answer would have to be yes. The terrible misunderstanding between Jesus and Peter (Mk 8:33), not to mention the programmatic temptations in the wilderness (Mt 4:1–11), would otherwise make no sense. Not only would Jesus have come to realize fairly well what the consequences of his teaching and prophetic actions would lead to; he would also have endured a profound inner struggle as he sought to remain steadfast to the path he believed God had charted out for him.

Jesus' Growing Sense of His Fate

It is difficult to say at what point during his ministry Jesus became fully aware that he would share the fate of the prophets. Perhaps he sensed it from the start, but then the enthusiastic beginnings of his ministry had pushed that prospect into the recesses of his mind. Or perhaps he sensed it under the impact of John the Baptist's death. Or perhaps he gradually realized that his life was in jeopardy the more resistance, opposition and downright hatred he encountered. Whatever the case, Jesus would have been perceptive enough to know that God's plan was going to take a turn which he himself could not fully envision. He might not have anticipated to what degree the kingdom which he proclaimed would eventually be connected with himself. Or to put the matter differently, the liberating power of the kingdom of God was somehow fused with Jesus' own faith. Being-with-Jesus would become the condition for experiencing that new graced reality which he knew and spoke of as the kingdom of God. God was making good on the divine promise to liberate, but that entailed the creation of a new historical reality, namely, a community animated by the prophetic Spirit of Jesus. Would Jesus trust the Father, and his own experience in the wilderness, to the end? Would he love the people of Israel enough (and, through them, all men and women) so as not to doubt his call to preach the kingdom? Would he continue to hope that the divine promise to Israel would be fulfilled, even when so many forces were arrayed against him? Would he love his sisters and brothers so strongly that he would not abandon them in their daily struggle to achieve freedom and justice?

The story of Jesus is most forceful when read against the background of oppression; conversely, it loses its energy where people have lost touch with their need for liberation. Those on the bottom cannot escape the fact of being oppressed, but they can suppress, or even be robbed of, any consciousness of what they are enduring, like the poor widow whom Jesus observed at the temple. Similarly, those on the top may not be suffering politically, economically or socially, but they can be blind to the links between their affluence and security, and the destitution and powerlessness borne by others. Salvation, or liberation, concerns both the rich and the poor, the strong and the weak, those on the top and those at the bottom of the social ladder. What is inevitable is not that the Messiah must suffer, but that all those who try to assist in the human struggle for liberation and redemption will be pulled into the pain and violence which occur whenever justice confronts injustice, good confronts evil, and grace confronts sin. Whoever gets caught in that elementary struggle runs the risk of rejection, betrayal, persecution, torture and death. Such is the price of sharing in the prophetic Spirit of God.

Did Jesus Know That He Would Rise?

One last clarification. Did Jesus know for sure that he would be raised to life "on the third day"? I raise this point, not to undermine anyone's faith in the gospel narrative as the evangelists have composed it, but in order to underscore once more the difference between the story and the "story behind the story." Because we tend to read the gospels literally, we are susceptible to being offended by any suggestion that things in the gospels might be otherwise than what they seem. This is a false or unnecessary danger, however. To repeat something we have already noted, our faith does not so much rest on the events which the gospels report but on the faith of the evangelists and the early communities who composed these narratives, just as their faith rested not so much on the parables and healings of Jesus, but on Jesus' own faith and the experience of God which lay behind them. The gospel writers bequeathed to us a story of faith. It was not fiction, nor was it biography or stenographic recording; it was a prayerful, imaginative retelling of the memories, legends and sayings of the Jesus whom they experienced as their Savior.

To answer this last question, then, I would suggest that Jesus did not know he would be raised "on the third day," as if he had been given a clear and distinct glimpse into the future. Above all, Jesus was a person who believed and trusted the God of Israel. If the God of Jesus' experience was indeed a God who made and kept promises, if this God stood truly on the side of the poor and powerless, a friend of those who had lost their way and the Liberator of Israel, then, Jesus would have had to believe, this God would never abandon the one who had allowed the voice of God to fill his heart and imagination. God would not abandon his Son. Jesus knew this with the certainty of faith, just as Abraham before him: "Abram put his faith in the Lord, who credited to him as an act of righteousness" (Gen 15:6).

Because the church's subsequent belief about Jesus was read backwards into the gospel story, Jesus sounds at times as if God had given him an advance copy of his life's script. Where then would be the need for faith? What would have been the point of his having to trust God? Jesus no doubt shared the belief, common in his time, that all the righteous of Israel would be raised at the end of time. It is also quite likely that Jesus expected the final restoration to be arriving soon (Mk 9:1); before long, he would again be eating and drinking with his friends (Mk 14:25). But the great event of Easter becomes all the more breathtaking if Jesus was communicating to his companions his own uncontainable joy and surprise, like someone who had just witnessed the creation of light. Unless we grant this, then the suffering and death of Jesus are in danger of being reduced to mere rites of passage.

The story of Jesus teaches us that God does not respond to the slavery and oppression suffered by men and women in some paternalistic way which neatly resolves all our problems for us. Instead, God assists us from within history, strengthening our will and our hands in order that we might throw off whatever yoke has been forced upon human beings. From a theological point of view, we might say that the principal spiritual issue facing us is not how God becomes real, but rather how the God *of Jesus* becomes real. And that happens as we love what Jesus loved, or as we share the same prophetic passion for justice, liberation and holiness which had been poured into him.

23

Jesus and the Church

"For the Son of Man did not come to be served but to serve and to give his life as a ransom for many" (Mk 10:45).

Perhaps nothing so unsettles a younger generation as the contrast (sometimes even the contradiction) they often spot between the person and message of Jesus in the gospel story, on the one hand, and the church of their experience, on the other hand. I say "of *their* experience," first, because young people often prove themselves to be excessively critical, and, second, because there are different experiences of church, depending upon what part of the world, or, sometimes, which parish one belongs to. Some local churches appear far more vibrant, youthful and evangelical in the best sense of the term than others.

A frequent and favorite target of complaint is the lifestyle of some clergy. As I listen to the tales, I cannot help but agreeing that, yes, sometimes ministers of the gospel forget Jesus' sayings about wealth, honor and service. But there is usually more to such tales than meets the eye. Human beings frequently scramble for excuses as a way of ducking their own responsibility to living out the gospel, and one easy way to avoid taking the gospel seriously is to appeal to the bad example of the professional religious class. The slightest defects and inconsistencies become magnified, usually to the point that the ornamentation of church buildings (and college grounds) comes under attack.

Indeed, the young people I have met have the correct intuition: to be in solidarity with Jesus is perforce to be in solidarity with those who are poor and struggling to make ends meet. And they may also be correct in asserting that Jesus had little in common with those who ogled the gold, silver and precious stones which adorned the temple in Jerusalem. When Jesus counseled the rich man to sell his possessions and donate the money to the poor, Jesus was on his way to Jerusalem; yet it never occurred to him to suggest contributing the proceeds to the temple treasury. But again, criticism can become the thinly disguised excuse which rationalizes away the gospel's challenge. I have watched undergraduates, after reading John Kavanaugh's *Following Christ in a Consumer Society* (Orbis Books, 1981), for example, become extremely defensive about what their parents own. And generally their first line of defense is the perceived failings of the ecclesiastical establishment. No wonder Jesus is remembered as having denounced much of the religious establishment of his day. Their bad example tacitly permitted others to take the kingdom of God less seriously.

The Lure of Power

The issue which arouses the most displeasure, however, is not the wealth of the church or its clergy, but the way the church wields power. A wise confessor once observed that of the three demons of sex, power and wealth, a person would be best advised to give in to sex, for at least through sex one might eventually discover the meaning of love, and thereby be led to find salvation. The satisfaction which wealth provides is fleeting. After a point, one becomes saturated with things and depressingly bored. Power, on the other hand, quenches a unique passion, namely, the desire to be in control of others. Many human conflicts quickly devolve into tests of power, of winning and losing. Hence the profound truth behind Jesus' observation that it is characteristic of godless people—the Gentiles—to lord it over one another: "their great ones make their authority over them felt" (Mk 10:42). This cannot be the case among the followers of Jesus, however. The antidote to the passion for power is humble service; the chaser is listening to and respecting other people's wisdom and experience in order to keep the trust one has in one's own experience from degenerating into arrogance.

In the church, there are people in positions of authority whose behavior comes across as immodest by gospel standards. In the name of safeguarding the integrity of Christian belief, they would silence the least dissent, mistaking criticism for insult. They seem to view themselves as protecting God and God's concerns, and since that is their goal, they presume divine permission to do practically whatever is necessary for their ends, even to the point of violating the Christian freedom of others and the gospel principles upon which that freedom rests. This is rarely done consciously, because they do not perceive the intrinsic contradiction of their actions. They would be as horrified to learn that they had become the scribes of their generation, as wealthy people would be to learn that they were the very ones who failed to notice Jesus as the poor lying outside their home. Young people are not offended because the church has its rules, but they are bothered by its refusal even to discuss certain issues. "Why," they ask, "is the ordination of women a closed question?" "Why can't there be married priests?" "Why do bishops have to be appointed by the Vatican instead of elected by the people of a diocese? The pope, after all, is elected." "Why can't any Christian celebrate the eucharist? I haven't met any priest who has more faith than my parents." And so on.

A Dangerous Question, A Dangerous Memory

I confess to often being at a loss about how to address such concerns, but I always take them seriously. One occasionally feels caught between loyalty to the religious institution one represents and being honestly open to the critical intellectual difficulties of people at the edge of church life. I am reminded of an anecdote which Gerald O'Collins recounted in *What Are They Saying About Jesus?* A young priest arranged an ecumenical liturgy in his parish in which Anglican youngsters of the town would join the Roman Catholic children, with the understanding that after the sermon the Anglican contingent would leave. But they stayed. The nervous priest found himself being approached at communion time by Anglican youngsters who had mingled with the Roman Catholics. He was explaining his predicament later to the bishop. When the bishop asked him what he did next, the young priest replied that he asked himself what Jesus would do in such a situation. To which the bishop, panic-stricken, exclaimed, "You didn't, did you?"

I know others who frequently resort to the same kind of reasoning. What this presupposes, of course, is that one has formed a fairly coherent and faithful representation of Jesus, which has been tested and discerned over a long period of time. The mature Christian, after all, ought to be able to say that he or she knows God in Jesus. One cannot appeal to the example of Jesus in order to justify everything, since there were attitudes and practices to which he was opposed. Yet there is a great deal which could be resolved quickly if we were free enough to ask the question: What would Jesus do under circumstances such as these? The reason why a bishop might find such a method to be disturbing is that it could easily subvert ecclesiastical authority. One recalls how foolishly the church resisted the practice of letting lay-people take communion in their hands. The ultimate casualty of such resistances is usually authority itself. When those in positions of authority lose perspective and throw themselves into defending practices whose meaningfulness has bottomed out, they run the risk of being dismissed as irrelevant to people's lives. As we saw, that is why the crowds greeted Jesus with such enthusiasm. He taught "with authority," and not like the scribes.

But what would Jesus have done about taking communion in the hand? He was, after all, a layman; and one needs only reflect for a few moments on the many confrontations with religious authority that marked his public life to realize how revolutionary those stories truly are. How could any Christian, let alone a minister of the gospel, ever take pride in, or boast about, having connections with people of wealth and influence? Why would any human being want to sacrifice his integrity, or his freedom to speak the truth, for the sake of pleasing or winning the approval of those in positions of power?

The question, "What would Jesus have done?" aptly frames the subversive character of the gospel memories about him. Would the Jesus who numbered women among his disciples have resisted letting them lead the eucharistic meal in his memory? Or forgiving sins in his name? Or bearing witness to the resurrection, like apostles? If being an apostle meant that one had been personally commissioned by the risen Jesus to announce the good news, then Mary Magdalene would qualify for the role. Would the Jesus of the gospel story have worried about whether all of his apostles remained celibate? Whether later generations should be allowed to take the eucharistic bread into their hands, even unwashed? Imagine the offense the disciples of Jesus gave to the scribes and Pharisees who "observed that some of his disciples ate their meals with unclean, that is, unwashed hands" (Mk 7:2). Some of Jesus' followers, in other words, were peasants and laborers, thankful for the fact that they at least had food to eat! What would Jesus have said to them, had they held out their hands at communion time?

Holding Power versus Being Poor

It would not be difficult to comb through the gospel texts and assemble the elements of Jesus' attitude toward power. The gospels of Matthew and Luke spell out somewhat the nature of Jesus' temptation in the wilderness; one of those demons was the offer of political power as a way to circumvent God's way of proceeding in the establishment of the kingdom. Occasionally, the disciples were mesmerized by power. Recall the time when James and John approached Jesus, asking the naive favor of seats on either side of him once he became the glorious (and victorious) king or messiah. They wanted to taste the thrill of being in charge of others and of "making a difference" to history. Jesus, however, was neither dazzled nor intimidated by those who wielded political power, the Pilates and Herods of this world, any more than he was afraid of those who held religious power and influence. He knew that the source of all power was God, and God's was the only power to reckon with, "the one who after killing has the power to cast into Gehenna" (Lk 12:5). Throughout the gospels references to service are numerous, because service is one corrective to the pursuit of power. Another corrective is letting go of riches. Since wealth often creates access to power, we can understand why Jesus' hostility toward money ran so deep. Thus, being poor with Jesus is the second corrective to the pursuit of power. In fact, the poor in spirit are free in a way that people under the spell of wealth and influence can never be. And, of course, from a theological perspective, the only "power" which can break the dominion of sin in the world is love. While this is not explicitly stated, it is the leitmotif of nearly all the forgiveness stories.

All of us need to feel free to ventilate our frustrations with the institutional church, which is inevitably going to happen in the course of our talking seriously about Jesus. No one can scan the newspapers for a week without running into at least one important issue facing the church today. Many people grow frustrated because they genuinely want to follow Jesus, but at the same time the institutional church, which they love, often delivers a counter-sign, and this makes them wonder whether the church has honestly bought into the story of Jesus.

Those who do, like the Salvadoran archbishop, Oscar Romero, appear to end up marginalized by the institutional church itself, almost as if they were ecclesiastical embarrassments. A heroic bishop stands a decent chance of being viewed as an aberration if he does not share institutionally correct politics. By insisting or pretending that it alone has access to the real truth of the gospel, the church effectively chokes whatever voices would utter a dissenting message. There is no place where the church needs to employ greater care than in the way its ministers exercise power. For in a community of disciples, the goal of all ministry is to empower, that is, to enable believers to develop their God-given charisms and talents for the service and upbuilding of the whole people of God. In fact, that is precisely what the story of Jesus does, provided it is fully told.

When the people of God become overly dependent upon ordained ministers, authentic lay leadership is gravely imperiled. Communities brought up to depend upon the priest can fall apart and become prey to pentecostal and evangelical sects, should they abruptly lose their clergy. The eucharist itself is so contingent upon the presence of an ordained male, celibate priest that, when priests become scarce, communities cannot celebrate the Lord's Supper. One wonders whether the church has adequately faced up to the accusation that the real institutional weakness is its inability to share power. If it fails to adjust itself to the legitimate aspirations of devout men and women today, its centralized power structure may follow the wake of the old Soviet Union.

The Gospel's Way of Being First

The one who truly possesses authority in the community of Jesus' disciples is the one who serves. The one who really wants to be first must become "the last of all and the servant of all" (Mk 9:35). Consequently, the effective leaders of the community will be those who have internalized the mind and heart of Jesus, the one who came to serve, not to be served, and to spend his life for the sake of others. Of course, "being first" in this case is not the object of unhealthy ambition; the disciple's only legitimate aim would be to imitate Jesus, not to lord it over others, or to be regarded by others as holy and special. The failure to make one's own the attitude of Christ Jesus (see Philippians 2:5) would reflect a person's being ashamed of Jesus and his words (Mk

8:38). We demonstrate that we are ashamed of him by behaving in ways which are fundamentally contrary to his example: honor and respect, yes; poverty and humiliation, no; teaching and issuing directives, yes; sincerely listening to and learning from others, no. Such behavior would be particularly reprehensible in the case of those who occupy places of authority among the people of God.

The whole people of God needs regularly to contemplate the final days of Jesus' life and the issues that came to a head when Jesus journeyed to Jerusalem for the last time. More than anywhere else, it is in the passion narrative, and the scenes immediately preceding it, that the early communities have preserved for us the sobering memory of what happened to Jesus and what he ultimately stood for. There is simply no way that individuals, communities or the institutional church itself can fake their way through the passion story. At some point, right from the experience of being betrayed, arrested and shamefully abused, Jesus is going to turn and face us, the same way he looked at Peter (Lk 22:61). With whom, finally, do we stand? Where, ultimately, do our loyalties lie? What have we done with our integrity?

24

The Cleansing of the Temple

According to Mark's account, Jesus arrived in Jerusalem accompanied by a throng of people parading ahead of him and crying out "Hosanna!" The scene certainly sounds like a royal entrance, and kingdoms, apparently, were on people's minds:

> Blessed is he who comes in the name of the Lord!
> Blessed is the kingdom of our father David that is to come!
> (Mk 11:9–10)

Jesus went to the temple area, surveyed things carefully, and then withdrew to Bethany, probably because he and his followers would be safer outside the city. The last thing authorities wanted to risk was an attempted revolution in Jerusalem, given the fact that so many pilgrims would have arrived at the city to celebrate the Passover, given the watchful eye of the Roman procurator, and given the fact that the basic theme of the Passover was Israel's deliverance from its enemies. A carpenter-turned-prophet from Galilee could spark a riot in an already highly charged atmosphere. Mark inserts a brief story about Jesus cursing a fig tree, because, at the time he was looking for fruit on it, it was barren, just like the temple itself. And then comes the scene of the cleansing. Given what took place, it is hard to imagine that Jesus acted alone while the disciples stood by, either timid (lest they later be arrested) or confused (wondering why Jesus would rashly take things into his own hands and provoke retaliation). Jesus' action is clearly prophetic, and it delivers an ultimatum: the religious leaders of Israel, charged with teaching and exemplifying the ways of God, had turned the dwelling place of God into a robbers' hideout. Strangely enough,

Jesus is not arrested. This suggests either that the temple police were napping, or that there was a sizeable crowd of people with Jesus. The political drama was escalating in intensity.

Jesus keeps going back into the city. He is accosted by the chief priests, the scribes and the elders, who question him about his credentials: "By what authority are you doing these things? Or who gave you this authority to do them?" (Mk 11:28) Jesus later goes on to tell the people a parable about some wicked tenants, which is just a thinly disguised allegory about the murderous and faithless religious leaders of Israel. Next, the Pharisees and Herodians attempt to entrap Jesus with the question about paying taxes to Caesar. Then the Sadducees approach him with their silly question about a woman with seven husbands in order to lure him into their religious squabble with the Pharisees over the resurrection of the righteous. Mark 12:38–40 contains Jesus' denunciation of the scribes, while chapter 13 predicts the collapse of the temple and all that it represents. "Learn a lesson from the fig tree," Jesus warned his disciples. If the leaf is sprouting, then summer has to be on the way; but if the leaf has withered, then what does this announce? The tree, the reader concludes, has to be dead.

Matthew's version fills out considerably the content of Jesus' denunciation of the scribes and Pharisees; it occupies nearly the whole of his chapter 23. Luke confirms that Jesus used the time in Jerusalem to teach, but only during the day, probably for security reasons: "at night he would leave and stay at the place called the Mount of Olives" (Lk 21:37). The gospel of John, however, places the cleansing scene much earlier in Jesus' ministry. John does not provide us with a glimpse into Jesus' enthusiastic proclamation of the good news as we find it in the other accounts. Rather, we are presented at the outset with a very forceful prophetic gesture, the sort of thing one would have expected from John the Baptist or Elijah, or one of the other prophets of old. Such a gesture would have carried enormous implications. If the cleansing did take place toward the beginning of Jesus' public life, then it would certainly have colored much of what was later to unfold.

The temple episode is revealing. It tells us something about Jesus' moral passion and conviction, for it would have required considerable courage and intensity of feeling for a Galilean layman to take on the religious establishment of Israel. In Jesus' eyes, the commercialization of the temple area was a clear violation of the respect due to such a sacred place. Yet beyond this, it was clear to him that one could not look to the religious establishment for leadership in a time of crisis. Within the tradition and memory of Israel, God was the great liberator. One would expect, therefore, that the religious leaders would have grasped God's way of thinking and judging, and that they would have seized the moment and assisted their people to respond to the great possibility which lay before them. At least, this would have been Jesus' expectation; but his experience proved otherwise. Looking for fruit, Jesus was bitterly disappointed.

Liberation theology is on the mark when it locates the center of Jesus' struggle and confrontation in the battle over justice. Reading between the cracks, as it were, the justice issues really do tie the mission of Jesus together. While Luke's concern with poverty and wealth is so pronounced as to make us wonder sometimes whether this was Jesus' issue or Luke's own, there is enough in the gospels of Mark and Matthew to confirm the idea that the kingdom of God was a kingdom of justice, and that Jesus unmistakably manifested a God-like solidarity with people who are poor and oppressed. This throws into sharp relief Jesus' emphatic rejection of the religious leaders, and his revulsion toward the cover-ups of their duplicity and greed. For the basic question to be asked was about whose interests they were really serving, whose well-being they really had in mind: the people's, or their own? Their behavior and their machinations would hardly have been surprising to anyone familiar with the prophetic tradition, however. Ezekiel had equally harsh words to address to the faithless shepherds of his day, too (Ezek 34). Because of the complicity of the religious leaders with the political power, and because much of Jesus' message would have threatened the economic interests of powerful and influential people, Jesus found himself on a collision course with the counter-kingdom.

It may have been that Jesus knew, deep in his heart, that his cause was doomed from the start. Or it may have been that his initial fervor and excitement wore off as he came increasingly face-to-face with cynicism and resistance. Or perhaps, growing up in a remote village of Galilee, far from the center of things in Jerusalem, Jesus was simply naive and innocent, unfamiliar with the harsh reality of the world. Whatever the background or the source of his frustration, the moment in the temple reveals immense anger on his part. It was much more than the well-intentioned actions of a zealous son defending the dignity of his father's house. It represented a calculated effort on his part to force the evil he had been encountering right out into the open: the temple scene was purely and simply a deliberate, violent confrontation with authority. It was hardly designed to invite the religious establishment to conversion. The gospel reader knows, of course, that this prophet from Galilee is God's Son. But anyone who was not "in" on that secret would have been challenged to make a clear decision about whose side they stood on, the side of God or the side of money. For the people who lived in (or off) the temple were, Jesus had implied, nothing but thieves. The scribes who devoured the houses of widows were proof.

25

A Disaffected Disciple

The fourteenth chapter of Mark opens with the somber fact that Jesus' life was in grave danger. The gospel then recalls a very moving moment when an unnamed woman approached Jesus while he was eating dinner and poured some extremely expensive perfumed oil over his head. We are not told what motivated her to do this, nor are we informed as to what she meant to convey by this lavish gesture. On a symbolic level, her act constitutes an anointing, as commentators have pointed out. In effect, Jesus has just been anointed as the Messiah of Israel, by an unnamed woman! According to Mark, Jesus accepted her gesture as a preparation for his burial, although the woman herself probably meant only to express her love and gratitude for something Jesus had done for her; what other reason would she have had to pour out such extravagance? It is possible, of course, that the woman was herself a truly faithful disciple who had comprehended more than the others Jesus' words about his approaching death, and perhaps, as Jesus remarked, she indeed did all that she could in anticipation of his burial, realizing there might not be another chance (Mk 14:8). Even in this case, the sheer value of the oil—nearly a whole year's wages—would render her gesture both reckless and excessive, unless we read it as the recklessness of love.

Whatever the reason behind her action, some others in the room reacted angrily. They were outraged over this foolish indulgence and saw it as a colossal waste of money. From poor, hardworking men this outburst would be readily understandable. When Jesus reacts by approving what she has done, they must have been scandalized, even horrified. How could Jesus, who had so boldly and consistently spoken out on behalf of the poor, and who had so recently drawn their attention to the plight of the poor widow at the temple, ever have permitted this? Such behavior on his part must have seemed radically inconsistent with the message they had been hearing and believing. When he went on to say, "The poor you will always have with you" (14:7), their indignation could well have turned to frustration and disillusionment. If they had been holding onto the hope that the kingdom of God would reverse everything and finally do away with poverty and oppression, they were going to be terribly disappointed. The poor, Jesus had just told them, would always be around. He then states, "wherever the gospel is proclaimed to the whole world, what she has done will be told in memory of her" (14:9). But the Jesus who utters these words has spoken out of character, since the Jesus of Mark had confined his ministry to the lost sheep of the house of Israel. At this stage, the notion of the gospel being proclaimed to the whole world would appear to be premature. This leads one to suppose that it was an early community, or the evangelist himself, who put these words on the lips of Jesus in the process of relating the memory of his final days.

Apparently it was this moment that pushed Judas Iscariot over the edge; he immediately resolved to strike a deal with Jesus' enemies. Mark does not say that Judas did this for the sake of money (John tells us that), but only that the chief priests promised him a reward for his help. In the gospel tradition, Judas is clearly the villain of the story. Given what he did, we readily understand why the tradition detested him. Judas had betrayed the friendship and trust of Jesus, the Son of God. In the popular mind, Jesus knows ahead of time what sort of person Judas would turn out to be, but he included him among the Twelve because the script had called for it. A traitor would be needed in order to hand Jesus over. However, this is to reason backwards, from fact to necessity: the event happened, therefore it must have been preordained. But that is not how the story originally went.

While it would be stretching things considerably to attempt to rehabilitate the image of Judas in the New Testament, as Kazantzakis does in *The Last Temptation of Christ*, it is important for us to pause and reflect about what might have happened to this disciple. Judas, after all, had been chosen by Jesus, just as the others were. There must have been a history behind Judas' attraction to Jesus and his desire to be one of his companions, just as there was for the other disciples. And Jesus must have recognized in Judas that zeal, openness, faith and eagerness which qualified men and women to be people of the kingdom. It might well have been that Judas' understanding of what Jesus both wanted and represented was seriously flawed; yet so was Peter's. And if Peter and Jesus exchanged words over the direction of his mission, what is to prevent us from thinking that some of the other disciples had similar difficulties with Jesus?

A reasonable way to account for Judas' behavior is to see him as someone immensely disappointed; Jesus had let him down in some critical way. As a result, Judas' decision to betray Jesus must have arisen from profound anger and confusion. He had staked everything upon Jesus, and now he found himself in the company of someone who was absolutely serious when he said that the chief priests and the scribes would condemn him to death. This was not the ending Judas had in mind; he was as intent upon the restoration of Israel as James and John were when they anticipated that Jesus, the Son of David, was at last about to take possession of his kingdom (Mk 10:37). The triumphal entry into Jerusalem, followed by the exciting confrontations with the religious leaders, must have ignited their messianic expectations, despite Jesus' previous instruction about service and powerlessness.

And yet it is not at all clear why Judas chose to approach the chief priests instead of simply withdrawing from the group and returning to his village. If he had grown totally disillusioned with Jesus, then why did he remain in his company so long? It surely could not be because there was money to be made (or taken). Why did he suddenly conceive such a resentment toward Jesus? Why did he go through the charade of eating the Passover meal with Jesus and the other companions? And why, finally, did Judas take his own life? Was it because he had never anticipated that his action would bring about Jesus' death?

Again, the gospel does not answer such questions, perhaps because the evangelists had no answers and thus were left guessing. Mark simply leaves us wondering about the terrible ambivalence Judas must have felt toward Jesus. It also leaves us wondering whether some important piece of information has not been omitted, something linking Judas, the religious establishment, and the radical nationalist movement of the time which saw armed resistance to the Romans as inevitable. Could it even be that Judas truly believed Jesus to be the Messiah of Israel, and that by precipitating a crisis he would be galvanizing crowds of supporters to rush to Jesus' defense and make him their king? This is pure conjecture. The only thing such a reconstruction has in its favor is that it illustrates what happens when disciples try to take matters into their own hands instead of trusting Jesus and staying with him. When the cause becomes more important than the person of Jesus, disciples run the risk of becoming ideological purists intent upon radical reform. But any attempt to force the kingdom of God is bound to fail. Even radical dedication to the church, apart from the Spirit of Jesus, becomes equally ideological and dangerous.

The basic issue with Judas may not have been greed at all (as suggested by Matthew and John), or that Satan took possession of Judas (as suggested by Luke). The basic issue might well have been failed expectations and disaffection, particularly the contradiction between Jesus' prophetic teaching and behavior, and his muddleheaded tolerance of a woman's extravagance. Judas wanted Jesus to be poor at a time when Jesus may have needed to feel the lavishness of human love. Judas' response to Jesus was insane. It is not impossible that he and some of the others were also jealous of the woman's spontaneity, although this can be no more than speculation. Yet one thing does become clear: there is no guarantee that each of us will remain faithful to Jesus to the end, or that we will not be deeply offended if he does something which does not conform to our image of him or the kingdom of God. Jesus and Judas were once friends and companions. The breaking up of their friendship had to do with money, and a rigorism that left no room for love.

The evangelists' contempt for Judas makes perfect sense, given the scenario they reconstructed about Judas' motivation. The Christian tradition's attitude toward suicide was probably colored by being associated with the dreadful action and fate of Judas. Today we are far less judgmental in this regard, given our understanding of mental illness and states of depression. The fact that Judas, utterly desperate and utterly alone, took his own life leads one to think that he never really expected that his action would lead to Jesus' death. On the basis of what we know about Jesus, however, it is not altogether inconceivable that Judas finally rejoined the Twelve. He never had the chance to approach Jesus to beg for forgiveness; but neither did the others, whose cowardice and fear were likewise cause for deep remorse. It was Jesus who came to reassure them. Who knows what happened when Judas had to face his risen Lord from the other side of the grave?

26

Of Weddings and Suppers

"The Son of Man came eating and drinking and you said, 'Look, he is a glutton and a drunkard' " (Lk 7:34).

In John's gospel, the first public "sign" Jesus worked was at Cana (Jn 2:1–11), and it consisted of rescuing a family from profound embarrassment: the wine for the wedding feast had run out. There is no doubt that this miracle, the beginning of Jesus' public "signs" (the term "sign" has a special meaning in the fourth gospel), is meant to draw attention to Jesus; it "revealed his glory" and enabled his disciples to begin putting their faith in him (verse 11). The other side of this story, however, is the occasion itself. In the background one imagines music, laughter, dancing, feasting, hand-clapping and merriment. Presumably, if Jesus had been invited, it was because the family believed he and his disciples would enjoy themselves. After all, one does not invite someone to a party who one suspects will feel out of place and stay seated the whole time on the sideline, carrying on serious conversation about heavenly things and muttering prayers under his breath! If Jesus was there, then he was part of the event, singing and dancing along with everyone else.

Weddings were special occasions in the life of a village. Families would have had to save some money in order to procure all the things needed, since the last thing one would have wanted would be for the guests not to enjoy themselves. In the days and weeks afterwards, the memory of the wedding feast would continue to linger in people's thoughts. In lives which were more or less ordinary and dull, where people could never afford to party often, and where, perhaps, most families would have had to struggle to survive from one day to the next, the prospect of a wedding feast would have been a source of excitement in the weeks leading up to it. The "sign" of the water-turned-wine might, perhaps, have had less to do with the glory of Jesus and more with the fact that in the kingdom of God, in the banquet of the poor, food and wine would never be exhausted. Following the intuition of the authors of *Un tal Jesus*, I would read the miracle at Cana less as an indication of Jesus' (or Mary's) sensitivity to a family in distress and more as a sign of God's seeing life from the side of the poor. Dostoevsky made the same point through one of the characters in *The Brothers Karamazov*: "Why, of course they were poor, if there wasn't even enough wine for the wedding. . . . Indeed, was it to increase the wine at poor weddings that he came down to earth?"

On numerous occasions, the gospels recount scenes of Jesus at table. Eating, after all, is a basic human activity. When the son of the prodigal father returns, the father throws a huge party to celebrate (Lk 15:23). After curing Jairus' daughter, Jesus instructs the parents to give her something to eat (Lk 8:55). When Jesus visits the home of Martha and Mary, clearly he came to dinner, because, Luke tells us, Martha was busy about serving (Lk 10:40). Upon reaching Jericho, Jesus encounters Zacchaeus, a rich tax-collector, perched in a tree and immediately sets off to his house, presumably to eat (Lk 19:5–7), thereby confirming his reputation as one who welcomes sinners and takes meals with them (Lk 15:2). Pharisees, too, invited him to their homes for dinner (Lk 11:17, 14:1). Jesus' final hours with his disciples were spent at a supper, and after the resurrection the two disciples on their way Emmaus recognized Jesus at the dinner table, when he broke bread (Lk 24:30). "The kingdom of heaven," we read in Matthew, "may be likened to a king who gave a wedding banquet for his son" (Mt 22:2). And, of course, we are told early in the story, that there was so much activity at the house in Capernaum that the pressing crowds made it impossible for Jesus and his disciples to eat (Mk 3:20), which must have frustrated the conscientious efforts of women like Peter's wife and mother-in-law to feed them (it must have irritated the hungry disciples as well).

Behind all of this, the reader has to hear the background noise: the clattering of pots and pans, the sounds of kettles hissing or the spattering of grease, the loud talking of the women as they cut and dice vegetables and meat, the antics of children running in and out, the banging of bowls and cups being set on tables, and so forth. Then there are the various aromas of oils and spices, fat dripping into a fire, or bread baking in an oven. There is the more distant preparation on the part of those working in the fields, or tending herds of sheep and goats; there is the raising of a few domestic animals, chickens for their eggs and perhaps a cow for its milk. There is the more proximate preparation of those who visit the marketplace each morning in search of fresh produce from the surrounding countryside. All of this imagery appears in the cracks between verses in the gospels. Jesus makes a passing reference to the father who would never hand his child a scorpion instead of an egg, or to the sort of song children might be singing in the market place, or to the farmer sowing his seed, or to shepherds, or to a family with nothing in its pantry when a guest arrives late at night (Lk 11:5–8), or to the rich man's bountiful harvest (Lk 12:16).

Everyone Has to Eat

The prominence of meal-taking as a setting within which Jesus meets people emphasizes the social aspect of eating together: it is a natural time for human beings to come together, relax and converse. It also calls our attention to the simplicity of the lives of the men and women who appear in the gospels. Their days are organized around elementary human activities, such as planting, harvesting, going to market, preparing food and eating. But the prominence of food imagery further suggests that many people of Jesus' day thought of little else, precisely because for many of them food was not abundant. Jesus' disciples, the story tells us, plucked grain on the sabbath, because they were hungry. The widow at the temple dropped into the treasury all she had to live on, and she was poor. The poor Lazarus lies hungry outside the door, while the rich family dines splendidly within (Lk 16:19–20). The scribes were denounced because they "devour the houses of widows," which effectively kept such women both hungry and impoverished. Bartimaeus was the blind man who sat on the outskirts of the Jericho road, begging; how else could he survive? Once, when Jesus was leaving Bethany, Mark tells us, Jesus was hungry (11:12). Then, of course, there is the verse from the Lord's prayer itself: "Give us each day our daily bread" (Lk 11:3). This verse does not take on its full significance apart from the experience of men and women who are unsure where their next meal is coming from. The later instruction about not worrying over what we will eat (Lk 12:22) only makes sense if the evangelist, at that point of the story, has envisioned Jesus addressing followers who have some resources at their disposal. One can give the rich this message about not being anxious, but Jesus could never have delivered such a message to the poor. The same point holds true with respect to fasting. Fasting is not a practice Jesus would have recommended to people who are perpetually hungry.

The category of food (and all that is connected with it) is one of the most strikingly humanizing elements in the story of Jesus. The kingdom of God is associated with mustard seeds, with wheat flour and yeast (Lk 13:21), with new wine, with wedding feasts and great banquets. Nothing so quickly establishes the humanity of people as our picture of them eating and drinking, chewing and swallowing, talking and digesting, passing dishes and helping oneself to bread, or fruit, or a piece of meat, or responding to a request for a dish outside one's reach. The wider context of the preparing and serving of meals, not to mention the cleaning up afterwards, is all part of the human condition which each and every one of us knows. To remember Jesus, therefore, in the situation of eating with people is very important. There was nothing rarefied about those episodes in his life. We do not find him, for example, ensconced in the dining room of some rich and powerful people, where no one can reach him. The sinful woman of the gospel story who rushes to his feet proves that (Lk 7:36ff.).

Around Jesus there was all the normal noise and activity which mark the preparing and taking of meals everywhere, the sounds of children, the typical approachability of ordinary men and women in their homes at supper time. To be sure, much of the gospel imagery reflects an agrarian society, where soil and crops, rainfall and harvest, storage barns and marketplaces feature into the warp and woof of daily life and conversation. But however incidental these features are, they underscore once again the humanity of the gospel as a story which is really about human beings and their lives, about Jesus and his life, and about the kingdom of God as a reality rooted in this world. The European theologian Edward Schillebeeckx noted that being sad in Jesus' company was simply impossible, and the proof was that the disciples of Jesus did not fast: "Jesus' presence becomes a living dispensation from fasting and mourning" (*Jesus: An Experiment in Christology*, p. 302). I would add that the same line of reasoning should be extended to Jesus' presence in the Spirit today, especially to his presence among the poor. Whatever fasting well-to-do communities undertake only makes sense to the degree that their experience of being hungry, intentionally and temporarily, enables them to enter into deeper solidarity with those whose fasting is both unintentional and daily. Otherwise, at least from a gospel standpoint, there appears to be no merit in going hungry.

The Problem Was Not the Food, but the Company

Two final points ought to be added. Jesus is remembered, not just for his un-prophet-like behavior of frequent meal-taking, but, to make matters worse, for sitting down at the dinner table of sinful people. Recall the time when Jesus, reclining at table in some Pharisee's home, was approached by a tearful prostitute. Jesus' host thought to himself, "If this man were a prophet, he would know who and what sort of woman this is who is touching him" (Lk 7:39). Genuine prophets, in other words, would have enough self-respect not to let themselves be found in the company of sinners. The scribes and Pharisees later complained, "This man welcomes sinners and eats with them" (Lk 15:2). What is important about this behavior is the signal Jesus was giving. If Jesus accepted sinful men and women, and felt comfortable in their company, then so does God. For all practical purposes, table fellowship thereby becomes a reconciliation rite; it points directly to God's readiness to accept human beings with all the messy complexities of their lives, provided, of course, they can acknowledge their needs, their inadequacies, their frail resolutions and their failed efforts.

This was a feature about the kingdom of God that righteous people found hard to understand. For the Pharisees, one does not eat with sinners because that would imply a tolerance of their unrighteous behavior. For Jesus, God tolerates all of us, the righteous and unrighteous alike. To have a meal at God's table is to be well on the way toward reconciliation, since one cannot take a meal with someone and simultaneously be that person's enemy. On the part of Jesus and his contemporaries, such a breach of etiquette would have been unthinkable. One consequence of this is that eating together (taken in its full social meaning) reconciles people. What took place when Jesus was actually present at table can continue to happen whenever his disciples, in their own homes and around their own tables, remember the example Jesus set. Our own tables can become God's table, provided that we, too, are leading lives which are oriented toward the kingdom of God.

Secondly, there is a marvelous text in Luke's gospel which implies that wealthy people become righteous in God's sight when they invite the poor, the lame and the crippled into their homes for lunch or dinner (Robert Karris calls them "the handicapped of society" in *Luke: Artist and Theologian* [Paulist Press, 1985], p. 62). In view of the ancient prejudices against human beings with physical defects (see Leviticus 21:17–23), Jesus' words carry a double cutting-edge and assume truly prophetic tones. Having been invited to a banquet, Jesus seized the occasion to lecture his wealthy host about how rich people might manage to crawl through the eye of a needle. Not only must they learn to invite the poor into their homes, who cannot pay them back by inviting them to share a meal with them; the well-to-do must also learn how to recline at table with the handicapped of society, if they want to understand what eating in the kingdom of God is all about.

For Jesus, every meal, no matter how ordinary, was somehow sacred, because it foreshadowed the day when all of God's daughters and sons would be able to sit together at a common table. Those who complained because Jesus ate with sinful people never grasped what sort of God the God of Israel was. Jesus sat at table with sinners because that is exactly what God would do, and God would do it because the only thing which could truly estrange someone from him would be the refusal to take one's seat alongside the others whom God had also invited to banquet in the kingdom. The presence of sin in a person's life would never have prevented Jesus from being at table with him or her and even sharing food from the same plate. Nor, apparently, would the presence of sin keep God from seating people at the feast in the kingdom. But first they had to be willing to accept the invitation, an invitation easily declined if one does not approve of the table fellowship.

27

The Last Meal

Everything which we have said about table-fellowship and the dynamics of meal-taking needs to be kept in mind when we come to the account of Jesus' final meal with his disciples. For us, Jesus' last supper with his companions is understandably pulled forward into the orbit of the cross, rather than backwards into his public ministry. Yet undoubtedly Jesus would have thought back that night to the endless occasions when he and they ate together. How many memories must have coalesced in his mind when he said, "I shall not drink the fruit of the vine again until the day when I drink it new in the kingdom of God" (Mk 14:25). Indeed, the truth was that they had often drunk together, so much so that the more ascetically minded had accused him of being a drunkard, and so unlike the great prophet John. John, whose baptism the religious leaders rejected, had at least behaved like a man of God!

The disciples, for their part, probably had no inkling that the end was in sight. They might still have interpreted Jesus' words to mean that the kingdom and triumph were just around the corner, and that shortly they would all be feasting and drinking together. Much later, whenever they would gather to celebrate a meal in his memory, they, too, must have recalled the many times when he and they ate together. There must have been much conversation, laughter, and, on occasion, heated arguments. They would have recalled and retold many of the things which had happened around the dinner tables of people who had invited them into their homes, especially the tables of those whom righteous folks regarded as unclean and sinful.

The gospel accounts of the last supper form part of the passion narratives and represent some of the most ancient gospel traditions. A close reading would confirm that this portion of the gospel story achieved its compactness from being recounted regularly, ever since the earliest days of the community. Most of us connect the last supper with the origin of the sacrament of the eucharist ["eucharist" comes from a Greek word which means "to give thanks." It is associated with Jesus' action of blessing, or giving thanks to God for, the gifts of food and drink.] The importance of the meal is often explained in terms of the historical justification for the church's primary liturgical practice. It is quite possible that the words of Jesus at the last supper have been scrutinized more closely than any other words in the Bible as a result of the church's efforts to present and defend its belief that Jesus is truly present to his community under the form of bread and wine. The phrases "This is my body" and "This is my blood" have been interpreted to be Jesus' perduring promise to remain really present in the church. The "is" in these texts means fully, really and substantially present. The best gloss or commentary on the eucharistic words of Jesus at the last supper may well be the sixth chapter of John's gospel, where John constructs Jesus' discourse on the bread of life. The text from John expresses the community's faith in the eucharist in terms which are scriptural, not philosophical. None of the tradition's subsequent theological speculation about the eucharist surpasses John 6.

Eucharist and the Forgiveness of Sins

Still, our understanding of the sacrament of the eucharist can never be separated from the connection which Jesus draws (in Matthew's account) between the bread being broken and the cup being shared, and the breaking of his own body for the forgiveness of sins. The forgiveness of sins, we have already commented, is the gospel's shorthand formula for expressing the full liberation of human beings from all that oppresses them. Such liberation (or redemption, or salvation) is first and last the work of God. To say only God can forgive sins is to state the truth that God alone can set human beings fully free. At the same time, God has entrusted this power to us, which is why the risen Jesus explicitly commissions his disciples to forgive sins. In fact, the mission to forgive sins must have been implied even on the earlier occasion when Jesus sent them out with authority over unclean spirits, healing people, preaching the nearness of the kingdom of God and repentance, even, Matthew tells us, cleansing lepers and raising the dead (Mt 10:7). For if the disciples were going to preach repentance, they must also have been able to reassure people of God's forgiveness.

In the accounts of Luke and Mark, Jesus associates the cup of wine with his blood, which now becomes the blood of the covenant poured out "for many," that is to say, for all people (Mk 14:24); Luke says, "for you" (Lk 22:20). In either case the covenant encompasses the divine promise to liberate the people of Israel, and now it further embraces all the peoples of the earth. The theme of freedom and deliverance is underscored by the fact that the final supper takes place during the week of the Passover, the annual Jewish feast commemorating Israel's miraculous deliverance from the hand of Pharaoh. The bread that Jesus was breaking was the unleavened bread of the Passover meal, the bread which the Israelites ate as they hastened to leave Egypt. Ever after, the Christian community's use of unleavened bread would serve to recall the night when God began Israel's great deliverance:

> "Keep, then, this custom of the unleavened bread. Since it was on this very day that I brought your ranks out of the land of Egypt, you must celebrate this day throughout your generations as a perpetual institution" (Ex 12:17).

Thus the eucharistic bread forever became the bread of liberation and freedom. In Jesus' eyes, the old covenant was about to be replaced by a new covenant sealed with his blood. The God of the old was the God of the new: the same God is involved, without change.

The Taking Away of Sin as Liberating Men and Women from All That Dehumanizes Them

While the later eucharistic tradition tended to associate Jesus with the paschal lamb and sacrifice, the dominant motif of the Passover was deliverance. The fact that lamb was on the menu was clearly subordinate to the reality which the Jewish community was celebrating, namely, God's leading the revolt of his people against oppression, slavery and exploitation. Today we refer to such things as social sins, that is, the inhuman forces and values which have infected the structures and institutions of society. The blood of the lamb on the doorposts of the Jewish dwellings directed the destroyer to "pass over" the families of Israel and slay the first-born among the Egyptians. Even then, the accent of the story does not fall on the note of Egypt's punishment but on Israel's dramatic experience of being set free from the power of social sin and injustice. As far as our understanding of the eucharist is concerned, therefore, the implication would be that Jesus' final meal with his disciples memorialized Jesus' great hope that God would deliver his people and inaugurate the kingdom. The stress falls, not on sacrifice, but on liberation from everything that deprives human beings of the freedom which should rightfully be theirs. The taking away of sin involves the taking away of all that injures or destroys our humanity, or the image of God that we bear.

A Failed Expectation

Jesus believed that the God of Israel—the God of Abraham, Moses, Elijah, David and Isaiah—was about to do something new. Jesus was looking at his approaching death in terms of the only theology he knew. He was associating himself with the categories of covenant, promise, liberation and sacrifice. Jesus' God had not suddenly turned from being Father to being vengeful, as if God were about to exact from Jesus the penalty for human sinfulness. God was about to fulfill the promise made ages ago, and that promise was intimately connected with deliverance from every kind of exploitation and oppression. If the old covenant had been sealed in the blood of a lamb, then the new covenant was also about to be sealed in blood. The timing ought not to be viewed as the result of a preordained divine plan; it was the result of historical accident. Jesus' end coincided with the season of Passover. To be sure, Jesus deliberately set out for Jerusalem; yet so did many other pilgrims at that time of the year. And who knows? Perhaps Jesus had been holding out hope that God would definitively intervene and establish the kingdom, maybe along the tempting lines that had been proposed much earlier:

> Then the devil took him up to a very high mountain, and showed
> him all the kingdoms of the world in their magnificence, and he

said to him, "All these I shall give to you, if you will prostrate yourself and worship me" (Mt 4:8–9).

The full weight of this scene starts to dawn upon us when the text is read in the light of Jesus' later wondering what might have been, had he chosen to follow a different messianic route.

But this was not going to be; the kingdom had failed to come as Jesus had hoped. The dramatic confrontations in Jerusalem toward the end, the provocative, indeed, incendiary action of cleansing the temple, Jesus' prediction of the temple's destruction and his words about final judgment, all served to bring his mission on behalf of the kingdom of God to a climax. The powers arrayed against him would bring everything that Jesus stood for down in a stunning defeat. What more remained, except to hope against all hope in the power of God to make good on the divine promise? Perhaps, through his death, God would find a way out, a way of offering human beings the divine promise once again. For everything Jesus had spoken about was contingent upon human response. The kingdom would not come, if men and women refused to change their hearts. Promises have to be heard *and* accepted; otherwise, they do nothing more than express the desire of someone's heart. Jesus found himself in the frightening position of the prophet whose word had been rejected, a word which had become inseparable from his own person. The one who bears God's promise also risks the bloody rejection of that promise by men and women trapped in their fear, their greed, their arrogance and their hatreds. How else could Jesus have interpreted all that had happened, and all that was about to happen to him, except in terms of the lamb of sacrifice and the history of his people's infidelity?

The Purpose of Remembering Jesus

Nevertheless, the fact that Jesus drew on the imagery of the covenant swings our attention to the unwavering confidence he had in the power and word of God. The fact is that Jesus believed that a new covenant, and thus a fresh possibility, was about to be established. The fact is that, according to one of the oldest traditions, on that last night he asked his disciples to continue to break the bread and share the cup in his memory: "Do this in remembrance of me" (1 Cor 11:24). What they were to remember was not just all that he had done or said among them; such a request on his part would have placed the community in the position of always looking backward, as if it had to keep the memory of Jesus alive for his sake. Indeed, it would have been demeaning, even selfish of Jesus to ask this. To remember Jesus would be to recall continually what still had to be done; hence the connection between his death and the forgiveness of sins. Jesus' instruction "Do this in memory of me" entails not only the ritual action of breaking bread and sharing the cup, but also selfless dedication to the unfinished task of human liberation and redemption. The forgiveness of sins would be the extension of Jesus' hope in the power of God to liberate and transform human beings into the future.

To remember Jesus, in other words, would be to remember the divine promise, which Jesus described as "the new covenant." If the events leading up to his arrest and execution were confrontational and deliberately provocative, then it would be natural enough to expect that the community of his followers afterwards would likewise find themselves from time to time on hostile terms with the powers of this world. No wonder we read in John's passion account, "If the world hates you, realize that it hated me first" (Jn 15:18). The remembering of Jesus would be dangerous; it would eventually bring the disciples to take the same risks which Jesus took, entrusting their lives and their hopes to the power and promise of God. The memory of Jesus would become empowerment for the future.

28

The Garden of Gethsemane

Then they came to a place named Gethsemane, and he said to his disciples, "Sit here while I pray" (Mk 14:32).

One place where the limitations of the old lives of Christ becomes evident is their treatment of the agony in the garden. What complicates their reflection is their Christology: the struggle in the garden becomes a conflict within Jesus as the God-man. The agony is intensified beyond belief because Jesus shares the divine nature; it thereby practically becomes a superhuman contest within the mind of Jesus, who shared the beatific vision, a sort of direct contact with God, from the first moment of his conception. Henri Daniel-Rops wrote:

> In that place, only a few yards from his friends, Jesus was more alone than he had been in the wilderness and here, in the hour when destiny took him by the throat, he experienced, in the most agonizing crisis he had ever known, the clash of the two natures within him (*Jesus and His Times* [New York: E. P. Dutton & Co., 1954], p. 481).

Daniel-Rops went on to say, "The essential quality of the scene is not its communication of almost unbearable distress but of a decisive acceptance" (p. 483). In other words, the verse in this scene which brings us to the heart of the matter is the line "not what I will but what you will" (Mk 14:36).

In the third volume of his study of Jesus, L. C. Fillion said:

> The word "agony" is St. Luke's, and no other word could so exactly express the terrible struggle which took place in the Savior's soul.

But, although the victim may for a moment be frightened and tremble, the sovereign priest, which Jesus also was, at once succeeded in calming the victim and inspiring Him with dauntless courage.

Then Fillion supplied the theological underpinnings of the scene:

> As our readers know, Christ's prayer in the garden of Gethsemani, aside from its salutary example for Christians of all times in their hours of trial, has a very great dogmatic importance, because it clearly shows in Jesus two distinct natures, the divine and the human, and also two distinct wills: the human will, to which so great sufferings were repugnant, and the divine will, which is that of his Father (*The Life of Christ: A Historical, Critical, and Apologetic Exposition* [St. Louis: B. Herder Book Co., 1929], vol. 3, pp. 443, 445).

Clearly, Fillion has focussed our attention upon the person of Jesus, which is altogether appropriate, but by presenting the scene in such dogmatic terms, the same idea which draws us in also excludes us from relating to Jesus' experience.

To complete this sampling, we might consult the second volume of Ferdinand Prat's work (which I had plowed through during my second year of college). He has the following comment to make about this scene:

> The agony in the Garden of Olives is, with the temptation on the Mount of Quarantania, perhaps the most frightening mystery of Christ's life. That the Saviour suffered from hunger, thirst, and fatigue, that he experienced heat and cold does not surprise us, because he willed to take a nature like to ours in all things except sin. But how could inner suffering have access to his soul, elevated to the beatific vision from the first instant of his conception? (*Jesus Christ: His Life, His Teaching, and His Work* [Milwaukee: The Bruce Publishing Co., 1950], vol. 2, pp. 313–14).

In each of these discussions, the experience of Jesus in the garden is complicated dogmatically by the christological assumptions of the writers. Since Jesus was both God and human, they reasoned, his struggle in the garden took on totally different proportions from those of any other human being. But by fastening on the agony as a conflict within the two natures of Jesus, their approach missed an important point. What happened in the garden is of a piece with the story which preceded it, namely, Jesus' mission of proclaiming the kingdom of God precisely as a kingdom of justice. The struggle is thereby presented in terms of the suffering which awaits Jesus; it neglects entirely the reason which brought Jesus to such a pass and the more likely cause of Jesus' anguish. What had happened to the kingdom? What had happened to the promise which he believed he had heard from God and which he boldly proclaimed, ever since the experience of his baptism and his clarifying search for the will of God in the desert? Was Jesus going to go the way of John the Baptist, prematurely and brutally silenced? What about the misunderstanding and rejection he had encountered along the way: had that been in vain? What had his fidelity to the voice he heard in the Jordan done to his relationship with his own family? Think of the confrontations, the healings, the demonic outbursts, the annoying dullness of the disciples themselves, the greed and arrogance of so many people. As the memories and experiences of the past few years crept across his mind, surely Jesus' soul must have been thrown into turmoil.

And then, of course, there was what lay ahead. In this respect, the lives of Christ were correct. Jesus would be offered a very bitter cup. It is hard to say, however, how much of this aspect of the scene reflects what Jesus actually envisioned, and what the community later came to impose upon the memory of Jesus praying in the garden. The conflict of soul would have to be heightened to correspond to the terrible fate which awaited him. A later tradition would portray beads of sweat pouring from Jesus like drops of blood; the struggle would have been so enormous that an angel had to comfort him (Lk 22:43–44). The author of the letter to the Hebrews would write, perhaps by way of reflection upon this episode:

> In the days when he was in the flesh, he offered prayers and supplications with loud cries and tears to the one who was able to save him from death, and he was heard because of his reverence (Heb 5:7).

Yet the fact remains that the garden scene underscores as little else does the humanness of Jesus, perhaps even too much so; the fourth gospel omits this "agony" (the prayer of anguish) altogether. (Donald Senior observed that, in a sense, in John's account Jesus had already done his preparatory praying at the last supper. See *The Passion of Jesus in the Gospel of John* [Collegeville: The Liturgical Press, 1991], pp. 47–48).

There is an echo here of Jesus' struggle of soul in the wilderness, after which, Luke had remarked, the devil left him "for a time" (Lk 4:13). The comforting angel which the gospel introduces in the garden scene recalls how, according to Mark, angels "ministered" to Jesus during his forty days in the desert (Mk 1:13). Perhaps they ministered, not by bringing Jesus water to quench his thirst and bread to satisfy his hunger, but by bringing him insight and consolation. They were the "good spirits" which one experiences in the process of discerning the will of God. For Jesus, both episodes, the prayer in the wilderness and the prayer in the garden, were moments of intense discernment of what the Father wanted of him.

One has only to read the gospel texts to pick up the notes of apprehension and fear in Jesus' voice as he prays to God to save him from what lay ahead. In John's account, Jesus prayed at the last supper: "I am troubled. Yet what should I say? 'Father, save me from this hour'? But it was for this purpose that I came to this hour" (Jn 12:27). According to Mark, Jesus' soul was full of sorrow, "even to death" (Mk 14:34), and according to Matthew, Jesus felt "sorrow and distress" (Mt 26:37). Having fallen to the ground, Jesus prayed, "Abba, Father, all things are possible to you. Take this cup away from me, but not what I will but what you will" (Mk 14:35). The distress of Jesus stands in vivid contrast to the sleeping disciples, who are still behaving true to form.

The Final Test: Can God Be Trusted?

Jesus' apprehension over what was about to happen did not arise, however, over some dreadful preview of the torture which awaited him. If this had been the case, then we might more likely be hearing a prayer for the ability to endure the next twenty-four hours. Jesus' apprehension most likely arose from his realization that there had been no decisive intervention in Jerusalem on God's part, despite Jesus' best prophetic efforts. The future grew suddenly horrifying because of his fearful awareness that now he stood utterly alone with God and his own faith. It is understandable that the scene in the garden gravitated toward the tragedy to come. For the evangelists, the episode in the garden had fallen into the gravitational field of the trials, the torture and execution of Jesus. For Jesus, that could have been a partial reason for the agony. But the deeper reason probably lay in the debate within Jesus' soul over whether God could be trusted to remain faithful to his promises. And the text which might confirm this view of things is Mark 15:34, "My God, my God, why have you forsaken me?" In terms of the Christian story, here is where we must locate the heart of Jesus' passion. This desperate prayer from the cross, the opening line of Psalm 22, suggests that at the very end Jesus' soul was facing the great nothingness of an empty promise.

In the end, I agree with Daniel-Rops that the essence of this gospel scene is Jesus' surrender to his Father's will. Yet the passion story presupposes that we know a little more about that "will" than has unfolded thus far, a little more, too, than even Jesus would probably have foreseen at that moment. Finally, Jesus' faith takes over, despite the dark forces now lined up against him. This surrender in faith will become absolutely critical for the Christian experience of God, since the faith of the community would rest upon the lived faith of Jesus. At this point, the question which nearly overwhelmed him was, perhaps, whether God could be trusted.

The reason why it is worth considering carefully this episode from the passion narrative is that it presents a sharp illustration of the drawbacks in the "old video," which we spoke of in the Introduction. The way in which many readers approach the various passion stories would conform, more or less, to the doctrinal presuppositions of the old lives of Christ. For them, the drama in the garden assumes gigantic proportions, akin to the great contest with Satan in the wilderness (whom Matthew referred to as "the tempter") with which the story began. A God-man was in pitched battle with the powers of darkness, but, as everyone knows, good was bound to conquer in the end. However, the overall dramatic effect of Jesus' soul-wrenching prayer in the garden should not be conditioned by one's familiarity with the events which follow, but rather by the events which had led up to that night.

There were no scribes present to record the words of Jesus in the garden (the sleeping disciples would have heard nothing), any more than someone could have recorded the dialogue between Jesus and Satan in the wilderness. The imagination of the gospel writers, or of the traditions they drew on, has supplied the words of Jesus in Gethsemane, as they tried to fathom what might have been taking place in the mind of Jesus that final night of his life. This episode provides a vivid example of why the church needs skilled storytellers, men and women schooled in the story of Jesus and the dynamics taking place behind the scenes, without some of the dogmatic prejudices of the past.

29

The Death of Jesus

Then they crucified him and divided his garments by casting lots for them to see what each should take. It was nine o'clock in the morning when they crucified him (Mk 15:24–25).

Few things disturb young people more than the message that somehow they were responsible for the death of Jesus, for that is what they usually take to be the meaning of the statement that Jesus died for our sins. Thus Paul writes: "For I handed on to you as of first importance what I also received: that Christ died for our sins in accordance with the scriptures" (1 Cor 15:3). In his letter to the Galatians Paul also writes that Jesus "gave himself for our sins" (Gal 1:4). Such statements leave them feeling guilty, if the intended sense of such texts is that Jesus died because of things that we have done. Upon reflection, moreover, many young men and women today find such statements to be incoherent, because they were not physically present at the time of Jesus' death. If the statements merely want to affirm that Jesus died as a *consequence* of human sinfulness, then they have no difficulty accepting their meaning, for the same thing could be said in every instance where innocent people suffer as a result of injustice, hatred, prejudice or greed.

The further idea that Jesus takes upon himself the sin of the world as the Lamb of God is utterly meaningless to them. How, they ask, can anyone take on himself or herself the sin of the world? Sin exists in the concrete; it exists in human thinking and acting, in human institutions and relationships; it consists of the evil which men and women actually do, or the good they fail to do; it resides in the human heart. But sin in the abstract does not exist. The notion of the "sin of the world" is simply too amorphous to mean anything to many people. Besides, why would anyone want to take on himself the world's sin? What would that mean? What sort of God would want such a thing? If the meaning of the statement that Jesus died for our sins means that his dying somehow liberates us, then perhaps there is a way of connecting the cross with freedom; but not apart from the resurrection. Theologically speaking, the cross means very little without the resurrection of Jesus.

Most of us are familiar with the major elements of the passion narrative: the betrayal by Judas, the flight of the disciples, Peter's denials; the hastily (and unjustly) summoned night trial by the religious leaders; Jesus' imprisonment and torture; the scenes before Herod and Pilate; the road to Calvary; the execution. The entire account reeks with the smell of rights violated, expediency, lying, and hypocrisy. There are false witnesses. There are trumped up charges. There is cruel revenge and the abuse of power. Crucifixion was a penalty the Romans reserved for political crimes, which suggests that Jesus was considered a political subversive. The term "Messiah" carried political overtones, and Jesus was paraded before Pilate as a messianic pretender. Pilate asked him, "Are you the king of the Jews?" When Pilate is made to appear reluctant to yield to the demands of the chief priests, according to John's version, the opposition points out that if Jesus claims to be king, then he is Caesar's adversary (Jn 19:12). Jesus' enemies then go on to insist, in the height of hypocrisy, that Caesar is their king (Jn 19:15). For John, the irony is that Jesus is indeed a king, but his kingship does not belong to this world. A political prisoner named Barabbas is spared the death penalty; Jesus is sentenced to die.

How to Explain His Death?

There have been many attempts to explain that behind all of this was great confusion about Jesus' true aims. He had never intended to present himself as a political messiah, as a king in any worldly sense. His mission, the explanation continues, was purely spiritual. It was to bring about repentance and conversion, inner renewal and personal holiness. The chief priests got it all wrong. Pilate, too, had completely misunderstood Jesus' real identity and purpose. Yet such efforts ultimately fail to account for why Jesus had the reputation of being a prophet. They also overlook the political implications of many of Jesus' actions and sentiments. Again, the irony of it all was that (again according to John's version) Jesus *was* opposed to Caesar: he had to be, because Caesar represented everything that God was against. Scholars have recognized that the passion accounts tend to let the Romans off the hook for the death of Jesus and shift the blame to the religious establishment of Israel. As the young church was trying to establish itself and win acceptance throughout the Roman empire, it had more to lose by continually telling a story where Rome was the villain than telling a story where the Jewish leaders were to blame. (See Paula Fredriksen, *From Jesus to Christ*, chapter 6.) On balance, however, both bear the blame; both were guilty of the death of the prophet from Galilee. Jesus had threatened the interests of both sides. A failed revolution would have brought the wrath of Rome down upon the heads of the religious leaders in Jerusalem. Literally, they could not afford to lose the support of their patrons, while the Romans themselves had very little tolerance for any form of public disturbance. Their punishment sometimes took the form of mass crucifixions. Even worshipping at the temple could be awfully unsafe, as some Galilean pilgrims had discovered (Lk 13:1).

In its historical context, the death of Jesus on the cross suggests that Jesus was executed for being politically as well as religiously dangerous, perhaps even a revolutionary. He posed a threat to the interests of those in power, and thus he was eliminated. *In the mind of Jesus*, his death would have been the tragic but predictable consequence of his prophetic call. Somehow, Jesus might have hoped, God might accept his death as a prayer or a sacrifice on behalf of the people in order, finally, to bring them liberation from all that oppressed them. To say this, however, does not mean that God subscribed to a theology of sacrifice; it is merely to say that Jesus would have fallen back on traditional, familiar categories as he tried to interpret his own experience. *In the mind of Jesus' followers*, his death upon the cross probably signified the collapse of his mission and the failure of his efforts on behalf of the kingdom of God. *In the mind of his enemies*, the death of Jesus meant good riddance to another annoyance from Galilee; it would also have meant that old scores had been settled. He who had usurped their authority in the eyes of many people, and who had embarrassed them in public, was now dead. The disgrace of death by crucifixion of one whom some had considered to be God's Anointed would have confirmed that all their doubts had been justified and all their resentment vindicated. *In the mind of God*, the death of Jesus would have confirmed that Jesus in all things behaved like a son who truly knew his Father: he was utterly faithful to his experience of being called and sent, he never renounced his trust or his hope, and he never allowed hatred or anger to consume his soul.

Appeal to the Old Testament

It is understandable that later generations of disciples would likewise try to make sense of Jesus' death. They, too, needed to locate the categories which would shed light on this chapter of the story, and naturally they turned to scripture. For example, several texts which would have hit their imaginations with considerable force were Psalms 22 and 69, and quite possibly Isaiah 53. It is quite probable, in fact, that these texts influenced the way the passion story was composed and handed on. Recourse to a passage like Isaiah 53 would have been impossible, of course, if the actual details of Jesus' death had not struck people as astonishingly similar to what is described there. Unlike the Christian martyr, Stephen, who gave a spirited defense of his belief before he was executed (Acts 7), and unlike the Jewish martyrs in the Second Book of Maccabees, Jesus remains astonishingly silent during the passion narratives in Matthew, Mark and Luke:

> Though he was harshly treated, he submitted
> and opened not his mouth. (Isa 53:7)

The following passage helps us to appreciate how Jesus' death could come to be regarded as suffering on behalf of sinners:

> Yet it was our infirmities that he bore
>   our sufferings that he endured,
> While we thought of him as stricken,
>   as one smitten by God and afflicted.
> But he was pierced for our offenses,
>   crushed for our sins,
> Upon him was the chastisement that makes us whole,
>   by his stripes we were healed (Isa 53:4–5).

Nevertheless, this text does not reveal what the death of Jesus was all about; it simply provides one perspective from which to view it. The notion of one person suffering vicariously for others has not been part of our cultural experience; it does not come from one of the schemes we normally use to interpret human reality. Even soldiers going off to war in order to defend the values and rights we cherish are not regarded as suffering vicariously for us. In fact, we might rightly regard anyone who would view his or her suffering in this way as having a martyr complex.

The Suffering of the One Becomes the Suffering of the Many

There is an important sense, however, in which human beings can enter into solidarity with others who suffer. This presupposes that one has deeply internalized being a member of the human community: in other words, that one experiences the world as communion. People whose spirit is in touch with the struggles and sufferings, the tensions and labors, the hopes and aspirations of human beings everywhere, are true contemplatives. They feel the joys and sufferings of their brothers and sisters; with them, as with God, there are no enemies and no strangers, only friends: indeed, only brothers and sisters, since all are children of God. Whereas the Isaiah text envisions an individual who apparently suffers on behalf of the many ["But the Lord laid upon him the guilt of us all" (Isa 53:6)], the solidarity approach would probably be to look at this individual as having been drawn into the experience of suffering of the whole human race.

What would illumine the death of Jesus for us, therefore, is not the category of suffering servant but of solidarity. The person who comes close to God will be drawn into God's experience of the world. The person who comes close to God experiences a God who is likewise in solidarity with us. This truth is the precondition for the Christian doctrine of the incarnation, and not vice versa. Because God is with us, as it were, it becomes possible to conceive of the Word of God becoming flesh and sharing our human condition. It is not that the suffering of the One became the suffering of the many, but that the suffering of the many had now become the suffering of the One. In other words, the suffering and death of Jesus could have meant for Jesus himself that he had been drawn into the painful struggle of all those throughout history who hungered and thirsted for justice, from the time of Abel until the end of the world. For the God of Israel had revealed himself to be the One who witnesses affliction, hears the cries of people and knows their suffering (Ex 3:7).

Clearly, the cross sums up the life of Jesus; Jesus crucified is totally unintelligible apart from the history which paved the way to this bloody moment. But the cross, as an event, has to be viewed in another context as well. The cross assumes its theological significance through the resurrection, because by raising Jesus from the dead, God was making an extraordinary statement about Jesus, about his death (precisely as death by crucifixion at the hands of godless people), and about everything which Jesus had done and taught. It is the resurrection which transfigures the cross, together with the whole of Jesus' life and person.

30

Jesus Handed Over
by the Father

In his New Testament study of the death of Jesus, Kenneth Grayston identifies a number of "explanatory myths" which Paul employed in order to shed light on how the death of Christ possessed saving power. Then he goes on to justify Paul's technique:

> Sooner or later it becomes necessary to ask, What kind of procedure is in mind when we say, for example, that the death of Christ effects atonement or has saving power? The best we can do is to say, "It is rather like the following situation," and then tell a story about human beings and God. The story, preferably containing traditional images with emotive force, is intended to provide not objective information but a viewpoint from which the death of Christ can be comprehended. I call these stories explanatory myths because the discovery of truth by means of imaginative stories was of great importance in antiquity (*Dying, We Live*, p. 342).

One of the troublesome expressions about the death of Jesus is the statement that the Father handed Jesus over. If atonement is not a particularly meaningful category for many people today, neither is the idea that God "delivered up" his Son for our sake. We simply cannot accommodate such an idea to our expectations about how parents ought to behave toward their children. The text from Paul, "He who did not spare his own Son but handed him over for us all (Rom 8:32a)," leaves our minds divided. On the one hand, we grasp that there is something in the text which is speaking to us about God's love. But on the other hand, we are left feeling uncomfortable with the implication that God not merely permitted but actually brought about the death of Jesus by "handing him over." The second part of the verse confirms our intuition that Paul is trying to tell us something about divine goodness: "how will he [God] not also give us everything else along with him?" (8:32b) The text, in other words, is about God's generosity and love toward us. The same point could be made with respect to a well-known text from the fourth gospel: "For God so loved the world that he gave his only Son" (Jn 3:16).

To resolve this problem of a mind divided about the way God is we need to do what Grayston suggests, namely, find the right story. That story is not going to supply us with new information, but it may provide a fresh viewpoint from which the death of Jesus can be looked at in a novel way. The following story is one which my students readily understood.

Suppose two very fine Christian parents had a child whom they raised in such a way that the child (let's say it is a girl) deeply and genuinely internalized the values and the faith of her parents. Further more, she is gifted with a charming personality, beautiful appearance and intelligence; she is respected and admired, wins many friends, and is firmly Christian. On graduating from college, she informs her par ents that she has decided to be a teacher because, she tells them, she loves what teachers do. The parents are pleased with her choice, as well as proud and delighted to see that she has made their values her own. She has been educated to be a woman for others. But then she informs them that she has decided to apply for a teaching position in an inner-city high school in an area known for its poverty, its crime, and its racial and ethnic violence, because, she says, that is where the need is greatest.

The parents gulp. They have applauded her decision to be a teacher, but the prospect of their daughter living and working far from home, in dangerous neighborhoods, has them frightened. Yet she is so determined and idealistic, her enthusiasm is both so refreshing and so typically her, that they reluctantly give their blessing. Nevertheless, every day she is away from home they are going to be anxious, ear nestly hoping and praying that she will be safe.

The daughter becomes a successful, beloved teacher who accom plishes a great deal. Her parents are happy, and they take great pride in her, but their worry about her safety never goes away. Families take to her easily; her warm personality has made her a very effective teacher. Then, one day, the parents receive the dreaded phone call. They are told that there was an "incident" at the school and that their daughter has been killed. They greet this news the way any devoted mother and father would: they feel shock, horror, profound grief and inconsolable sorrow. They also feel terribly guilty, accusing themselves for not having resisted strongly enough their daughter's plan to teach in such a dangerous place. They even begin to feel remorseful about the way they had raised her. If they had not brought her up to be so conscientious, so mindful of others, so sensitive to the needs of the larger world, so selfless, even so innocent of the world's cruel side, then perhaps, they tell themselves, she would still be alive. The parents believe that, in a real sense, they have been responsible for the death of their child.

In some way, maybe this is how it was with Jesus. God was his Father: Jesus had internalized God's own outlook on the world, as it were. Jesus "felt" the world and its needs the way God would; his selflessness, his ability to see other men and women as truly his sisters and brothers, his compassion, his zeal for justice—all of these he had acquired as a result of being in relationship to God. And when the course he took finally brought him to his death, one could say that somehow the result was God's fault. If God had not "raised" Jesus to be so much like the divine image and likeness, then Jesus might never have lost his life. We might then imagine the divine reaction to the death of Jesus to be one of profound grief and sorrow, even one of outrage over the circumstances which led to his death. But the human race needed to be taught; God understood better than any human parent ever could the immense need of human beings to hear and be taught the word of God. In some such sense, one can say that God handed Jesus over. God bears responsibility for Jesus' being the kind of human being he was.

When I think of the four missionary women from the United States who were slain in El Salvador in December 1980, or of my own brother Jesuits who were also murdered there nine years later, I cannot help but wonder about how their parents would have felt. The made-up story falls pretty close to the mark. Insofar as the Christian community raises its young people to be like Jesus and teaches them to make the gospel story their own so that they come to share that passion for the kingdom which led Jesus to embark upon his mission, then Christian upbringing becomes dangerous. It should hardly be surprising that one of the repressive strategies deployed by a number of governments and paramilitary death squads in Central and South America has been the terrorizing and killing of catechists, and the confiscation of Bibles. Men and women who have dedicated themselves to retelling the story of Jesus pose a grave threat to godless people.

PART FIVE:
NEWNESS OF LIFE

31

The Resurrection (I): Joyous Fear

The centerpiece of the church's proclamation about Jesus is that he has been raised from the dead. Although this part of the gospel texts appears at the end, the storyteller could well begin with Easter and narrate the story of Jesus backwards, as it were. With our knowledge of the ending, we could return to the beginning and tell the story the way the evangelists knew it. The advantage of this procedure is that it would avoid reducing the main part of the gospel story, which contains the bulk of Jesus' miracles, exorcisms and signs, into an apologetic or defense of the identity of Jesus as Son of God. Starting with the resurrection, we would retrace the major elements in the life of Jesus, right from the time of his appearance at the Jordan river, with our imaginations already attuned to the breathtaking sound of God's good news. That is, having been told about Easter, we start in the position of men and women who want to hear more about Jesus; we begin, in other words, as seekers or catechumens.

Paschal Fear

As sheer story, the Easter remembrances are rich in the elements of surprise, joy, victory, and the exhilarating freedom which comes from the gift of forgiveness. They convey a sort of evangelical fear, too. There may be times in our lives when we become afraid to do something because of our uncertainty over whether our efforts have been fully discerned (is there some concealed motivation lurking in our hearts that would eventually undo our efforts?). Or we may be unsure as to whether or not what we feel called to do really enjoys God's blessing (suppose we try and fail?). Yet what about another sort of fear, namely, being afraid that we are right? We have learned to live with failure; all of us have to reconcile ourselves with our errors and mistakes, and our lives are often replete with these. But what about success? Does the prospect of being right frighten us? What about the nervousness of suspecting that we may in fact be doing exactly what God wants of us, and that our decision to follow our intuitions is going to cost us a great deal personally? What then? There is the uniquely paschal fear of stepping into the unknown, of stepping into a future which, one now knows for sure, truly belongs to God.

After hearing the news about his being raised from the dead, the women (and, presumably, the disciples) were overtaken by fear (Mk 16:8). To be sure, it is possible that they were frightened by the strangeness of that news, in the way that the unknown typically strikes fear in us, just as the disciples were terrified at the scene of the transfiguration (Mk 9:6). Maybe that is why the women are reassured, "Do not be afraid!" (Mt 28:10). Meeting Jesus would have been like a tale from the crypt, as if they had been confronted by a ghost (Lk 24:37), which is likewise reminiscent of an earlier episode, namely, the night when Jesus walked on the sea (Mk 6:49). In John's gospel, the disciples are also overtaken by fear, but there it was the fear of being discovered and arrested by the religious authorities (Jn 20:19).

But it might be more plausible to think about what might be called evangelical or paschal fear, that is, the fear associated with the process of discipleship. The disciples would have grown fearful as the likelihood finally dawned upon them that Jesus was right, more so than any of them had ever suspected. His actions, his message, his way of living began to emerge in a very different sort of light. The rightness of Jesus' words and deeds, together with the promise of God upon which he staked his life, now posed a fearful logic: all that Jesus believed, and all that he did and represented, could no longer be read as something purely notional, as if to say, "That was Jesus; he had to do his own thing." It now included a terrifying "ought": if Jesus lived that way, then, after Easter, the inference which the disciples had to draw would be that they, too, had to live that way. What Jesus stood for must now become their cause; even the suffering and rejection which accompany those who inherit the prophetic mantle would become theirs.

The fear connected with the Easter story as Mark told it may have been the fear that Jesus had been proven right. One listens to the story, therefore, with immense interest, in order to learn what exactly Jesus was all about. One listens to the story with joyful trepidation, because the story of Jesus could very likely become the story of one's own life. It is a great blessing, and a source of lasting joy, to find oneself in the company of Jesus; but where might this being-with-Jesus take us? It is amazing how being in this position can affect the way one approaches the gospel. One reads the story with the somewhat nervous feeling that one's own future may be on the line. If there had been divine words accompanying the action of raising Jesus from the dead, they might very well be, "This is my beloved Son. Listen to him" (Mk 9:7). "Listen to him" means "listen to his teaching and learn from his actions." For us these words mean "listen to his story."

The Problem of Trying to Picture the Resurrection

Several years ago, I devoted one class period to surveying some of the current theological positions regarding the resurrection. The following class, one student reported that his mother had become very upset when he told her over the phone the previous night that they had just learned the resurrection never really happened. His attention had lapsed somewhere between my comment about the empty tomb and my explanation as to why some scholars maintain that the resurrection could not in principle be regarded as an historical event. The theological issue had turned on the customary historical criteria for verifying that something had taken place. In the case of the resurrection, there were no witnesses to whatever occurred on that Sunday morning; and because there were no witnesses, we have no historical basis for picturing what actually took place.

Subsequent attempts on my part did not improve my students' comprehension of the resurrection, because I was always attending to the theology of the resurrection, whereas they were endeavoring to picture what Easter morning looked like. In their minds, the unity of the gospel story seemed to break apart with the resurrection narratives; the evangelists no longer appeared to be following a common thread once they came to the Easter events. The picture, in short, started to go haywire. In John 20, Jesus seems about to ascend to the Father on Easter Sunday itself (chapter 21 of John reads somewhat like an appendix), whereas according to Luke forty days intervened (Acts 1:3). Mark apparently concluded his gospel rather abruptly, and on the note of fear: "They went out and fled from the tomb, seized with trembling and bewilderment. They said nothing to anyone, for they were afraid" (Mk 16:8). Mark tells us nothing about Jesus risen, while Matthew simply amends Mark somewhat. The women are both "fearful" and "overjoyed"; they do not remain silent, but rather announce the news to Jesus' disciples (Mt 28:8). While in Mark a "young man" instructs the women, and Matthew clarifies for us that the young man was an angel (who had also been responsible for rolling back the great stone), it is only in Luke and John that we find the fully-blown appearances of the risen Jesus. Yet, whereas the risen Jesus in Mark was about to head to Galilee, in Luke and John we find him in Jerusalem. And so on.

Nevertheless, the imagination can still pause over these scenes, however discordant they may strike us. One can try, as St. Ignatius Loyola does in the Spiritual Exercises, for example, to imagine what an encounter with the risen Jesus might have been like. Needless to say, this requires that one has been able to identify with the experience of the disciples up until the night of Jesus' arrest and through the moments of the passion story. Those who encountered Jesus risen already enjoyed a history with him. Whatever transpired between the risen Jesus and his disciples took place against that background, and in the days immediately following the crucifixion, they must have been plagued by the memory of how faithless they had proven when Jesus needed them most. Peter, in particular, would have been eaten by remorse and guilt.

Paschal Joy

One of the most heart-warming chapters of *Un tal Jesus* is its reconstruction of Peter's meeting with Jesus. The disciples are crushed and fearful, guilty and ashamed, and hiding in the cellar of a house in Jerusalem. They dare not go outside. Mary Magdalene has returned, hysterical, with strange news; the disciples are convinced that the pressure and tragedy of the last few days have pushed her over the brink. Peter and John slipped out and raced to the tomb. Finding it empty, they suspected that they were being set up by the temple police or by the Romans and fled in panic. John outran Peter, and so poor Peter, trembling with fright, was making his way back to the house when he was accosted by a stranger. As he is narrating the story afterwards, Peter is beside himself with laughter. In fact, he is laughing so hard that he can hardly speak. He reports to the others about his being followed, about his being cornered by a stranger who saw right through him when Peter denied that he was a Galilean and a fisherman from the lake, and protested that he was a pottery maker named Julian who had never even seen the water. The others chimed in, "What a coward you are, Peter!" And Peter exclaimed, "That's exactly what the stranger said: 'What a coward you are, Peter!' " Then the stranger smiled, and the smile, broad and bright like the sun over the Lake of Tiberias, suddenly broke over Peter's fear and guilt. From the smile and the laughter, he knew it was Jesus.

What is so fascinating about the scene is the laughter and the absolutely joyous way in which Peter tells his story. As days pass and more of the disciples meet the risen Jesus, their happiness is downright contagious. They sound and behave like men and women who have suddenly been let in on a great secret; they are living as if the world had suddenly been turned upside down, and they alone were the ones to notice how radically different everything looked. There is nothing sullen or vindictive about the risen Jesus, as we watch the experience of his disciples. At Easter we hear the laughter of God, and the invincible, jubilant conviction that the unfolding of the kingdom cannot be thwarted by the power of death.

As one reads through the various resurrection narratives, one finds a range of reactions: from fear and amazement, terror, disbelief, being troubled and doubtful, to great rejoicing. The reaction of the male disciples to the women's news was typical: it seemed like nonsense (Lk 24:11), perhaps as much over the preposterous idea that God would ever have entrusted such world-shattering news to the testimony of women, as over the news itself. Overall, however, the reactions seem to pivot on the notes of fear and joy. From the point of view of the story and the dynamics of following Jesus through one's imagination, there is the peculiar "joyous fear" which seems to be a part of the paschal experience. And that is something worth meditating on, because in the end it creates the interior freedom which enables us to follow Jesus.

32

The Resurrection (II): Resuming the Mission

The disciples, it appears, were not anticipating the resurrection of Jesus, despite the three passion predictions. Those closest to Jesus fled in fear and disgrace. It would have made no sense, then, for them to turn around and steal the body of Jesus in order to pretend that he had really been raised. After all, what would being raised from the dead have meant to the ordinary person? The ordinary person, even the disciples themselves, would first have assumed that they were being haunted by a ghost. Upon reflection, they might have drawn the conclusion that the general resurrection of the dead had begun and that the final age of the world was upon them. While it confirms the existence of eternal life, the resurrection of Jesus did not reveal it; everlasting life was something already believed in (at least by Jesus and many of his contemporaries). So too was bodily resurrection, as the religious debate between the Pharisees and the Sadducees shows. The resurrection does not automatically disclose the divinity of Jesus, either, since it was widely believed that all the righteous of Israel would be raised. Jesus was but the firstfruits of this general resurrection (1 Cor 15:20).

It goes without saying that Jesus assumed a special status after being raised from the dead, but the theological significance of the resurrection should not be gauged primarily in terms of the identity or status of Jesus. Rather, one needs to attend to what the risen Jesus proceeds to do: he rebuilds the faith of the disciples and he prepares them for mission. Community and mission appear to be the two concerns of the Easter Jesus, the one now definitively anointed with the

Spirit, the Christ (or Anointed One) of God. As a matter of fact, the ascension notwithstanding, the risen Jesus does not depart from our world or its history and retire to celestial glory. Instead, he becomes more deeply a part of our world, constantly leading us into new Galilees. On God's part, the resurrection affirms unambiguously the mission of Jesus and his oneness with sinful human beings, many of whom are poor, exploited and oppressed. The raising of Jesus from the dead, therefore, is about justice and the creation of the church. Easter prepares the disciples to step into the future with the Spirit of Jesus, proclaiming repentance and forgiveness in his name (Lk 24:47; Jn 20:21–23).

If Jesus believed up until his last fateful hours that the kingdom was truly imminent, he was mistaken. On hindsight, Jesus' words, "Amen, I say to you, there are some standing here who will not taste death until they see the kingdom of God has come in power" (Mk 9:1), appear embarrassingly unfulfilled. In raising Jesus from the dead, the Father was not confirming the apocalyptic worldview shared by Jesus and many of his contemporaries. They would have subscribed to this mentality as naturally as people before Columbus might have subscribed to the natural observation that the earth was flat. On the contrary, the Father had confirmed Jesus' teaching and his prophetic witness on behalf of the kingdom, for the kingdom of God as the kingdom of justice and holiness would remain "imminent for all time." In every generation and in every age, its advent would be contingent, just as it was in Jesus' day, upon the faith-response of men and women: Do they want the kingdom more than anything else? Are they willing to follow Jesus and to live in his company in order to see that kingdom become a reality?

The resurrection did not usher in a radical transformation of human society, but it did introduce something revolutionary into creation. The resurrection destabilized the everyday world by undermining its fundamental assumptions about the way things are supposed to be. All the evil in the world, collectively symbolized as the power of Death, cannot frustrate God's determination to liberate human beings from oppression. As his story is retold and relived, the mission of Jesus to bear witness to this divine promise and his service as God's Son of setting human beings free will unfold until the end of time.

One final caution. We have to be careful not to interpret the revelation of Easter solely as a divine pledge of a life to come. The mission of Jesus would be too narrowly conceived if it were cast simply in terms of "saving souls" from eternal death. Once one adopts that view, it will only be a matter of time before one begins regarding Jesus as the exclusive key to salvation, as if the Creator had determined that faith in Jesus would be the only route for humanity's entrance into heavenly glory. And this cannot be.

Obviously, there were righteous people before and after Jesus, men and women who placed their faith in God but who could never have had any contact with the gospel. So long as salvation is construed in other-worldly terms, we run into theological problems about the salvation of the non-Christian. For behind such a view of salvation is a theological construction about the economy of grace and preordained divine plans which sew up the mystery of redemption in Jesus; whatever "grace" enters the world is the "grace of Christ" and comes through him. But if the mission of Jesus as God's Anointed concerns this world; if the full, integral liberation of the human being has to do with history in all its concrete details; then one's understanding of the mission and identity of Jesus will be significantly altered. One ought not elevate Jesus into the role of being a spiritual Messiah whose power and mission extends simply to all *souls*. There has to be a broader conception of what bondage and oppression mean.

There is nothing which prevents men and women from being with God apart from Jesus (the exclusivist faith claims of the fourth gospel notwithstanding); but there is an experience of God which is unique to being-with-Jesus. What this experience entails and leads to cannot be explained without telling his story.

33

Two Easter Stories from Mark

Unlike the other evangelists, Mark apparently ended his gospel without including any episodes about the risen Jesus' encounter with his companions. He simply ends with the story of the empty tomb (16:1–8). If this was intentional (and not merely the result of an accidental tearing away of his manuscript's final verses), then the narrative effect is actually very interesting. Mark is provoking his readers into thinking about what exactly the resurrection means for them; he does not want them distracted by what sort of bodily appearance the risen Jesus had assumed. It might be said, however, that since the whole of the gospel was composed from the perspective of Easter faith, Mark's entire narrative is one long Easter story. From time to time, that perspective breaks into the narrative. It is important to note this, because the alert reader may have found himself or herself jarred by an intrusion of puzzling elements into what had been sounding more or less like a straightforward account of what was going on historically in the life of Jesus. Two scenes in particular illustrate this. Both occur on the Sea of Galilee: the calming of the storm in chapter 4 (which we have already adverted to) and the walking on the water in chapter 6.

The First Appearance (Mk 4:35–41)

Both stories contain some unusual features. In the first story, Jesus is sound asleep on a pillow while his disciples are screaming, the winds are howling, and the waves are crashing over the side of the boat. We should not think that Jesus is absolutely exhausted from his labors, and that this explains why he could remain asleep. Nor should we think that Jesus is play-acting at being asleep in order to give his disciples another test in the practice of faith. Imagine a father holding his frightened five-year-old son by the hands from the roof of a skyscraper, in an attempt to teach the child a lesson about trusting his parent. "You have to believe," the father says, "that I would never drop you." Such behavior would be insane as much for a human parent as it would be for God. Whatever the testing of faith may mean, it does not mean God's toying with our fears.

To appreciate what Mark as a storyteller has done we need to recall that he was not writing for the first disciples themselves, but for the generation of a later day. He has shaped his story to meet the needs and address the concerns of people who would quickly identify with the experience of being in grave peril. The disciples become characters of a story which probably had little to do with an actual situation from the time they spent with the historical Jesus. The Jesus who "sleeps" is the Jesus whom the community approaches through prayer and faith, who at this moment feels absent. An individual, or a community, threatened with disaster is wondering where Jesus is and prays, "Lord Jesus, don't you care that we are perishing?" In other words, Mark is trying to help answer a question: How does one experience the presence of the risen Jesus when one is in the middle of some particularly fearful situation? As far as Mark is concerned, Jesus is there, in the "boat," even though he seems not to be there at all. Thus, Mark reassures us from his own faith, we have no reason to be terrified. The one "whom even wind and sea obey" is the risen Jesus. And if it should happen that the boat goes down, then at least the companion of Jesus has the consolation of dying with him.

A Second Appearance (Mk 6:45–52)

The second episode also contains an unusual feature. Jesus has withdrawn to a mountain and his disciples are far out on the sea in the middle of the night. Coming down from the mountain or hillside, he arrives at the shore only to "see" them being tossed about and rowing strenuously against the wind (6:48). Either the disciples are not far from shore, or else the "seeing" has to do with the fact that Jesus, now risen, always "sees" his companions, particularly when they find themselves in desperate circumstances. The odd thing here is that Jesus walks across the water in order to join his struggling companions, which leads the terrified disciples to believe that they are about to be boarded by a ghost. The note of fear and the failure to recognize Jesus are both characteristics of the resurrection stories which we find in the other gospels. This suggests that Mark may have inserted his Easter stories at earlier points in the narrative than the other evangelists do. The Jesus who says, "Take courage, it is I, do not be afraid!" is not unlike the Jesus who would also say, "Peace be with you" (Jn 20:19 and Lk 24:36). Mark explains that the disciples missed the point (once again) because their hearts were hardened (Mk 6:52), while Luke reports something similar in one of his resurrection episodes:

> But they were startled and terrified and thought that they were seeing a ghost. Then he said to them, "Why are you troubled? And why do questions arise in your hearts?" (Lk 24:37–38)

Hardness of heart, we might conclude, is what prevents the disciples in Mark's gospel from recognizing the presence of the risen Jesus in their midst. For that reason, the risen Jesus must continue to open their ears and their eyes, something which Mark graphically describes in the stories of the tongue-tied deaf man (7:31–37) and the blind man of Bethsaida (8:22–26). Jesus' question "Do you not remember?" is addressed as much to the later generations of readers as it was to his first companions. In effect, Mark is asking us to remember the story of Jesus when we, the community of a later age, find ourselves in nearly impossible situations, such as being called upon to provide food for vast multitudes of people, or to confront resistant demons, or to face tyrants, or to do battle against injustice, or, against all odds and prudence, to take the side of desperately marginalized and oppressed people. There is no situation, no matter how terrifying or desperate it might be, where Jesus is not with his community to strengthen and guide them as they interpret the wonderfully liberating memories of the God of Israel. Jesus always "sees" his disciples, even when they feel most alone, adrift and in danger.

34

A Note on Freedom in Paul

"For freedom Christ has set us free" (Galatians 5:1).

Paul never knew the historical Jesus the way Peter, James, John, Mary of Magdala and the others did. Perhaps this helps to account for why he concentrates so heavily on the death and resurrection of Jesus in his "gospel." Paul was among the very first Christians to reflect extensively upon the death of Jesus in symbolic terms, but at the expense of underestimating the history which preceded it. To a large degree, Paul's Christology is autobiographical. We learn a great deal about Paul's Jesus, that is, about Jesus through Paul's experience of him. And central to that experience was Paul's own record of suffering, which he had incurred as a result of his fierce dedication to the gospel. That experience of rejection, betrayal, imprisonment and torture confirmed for him that the pattern of Jesus' life (which was the cross) was also being traced over his life.

As Paul attempted to unfold the Christian mystery, he appealed to the symbolic level of human experience, and in particular, to the parallel which he saw between Christ and Adam. Just as in Adam all died, so in Christ all came to life. "Adam," in short, became a major interpretative key for deciphering the significance of Jesus' death. Through Adam, sin, death and slavery enter the world; through Christ, on the other hand, grace, life and freedom are given. In Adam, all are slaves; in Christ, all become daughters and sons. It may be worth pointing out that one can appreciate the richness Paul came to discover in the Christian mystery without subscribing to the historical existence of Adam. (In the same way, one can believe in Jesus' oneness with the Father without necessarily subscribing to the metaphysical notion of preexistence, and one can affirm that Jesus is God's Son without recourse to the category of virginal conception.) Adam serves as a symbolic counterpoint within Paul's theologizing about the death and resurrection of Jesus, but the purpose behind this theological reflection is not to wax notional or abstract. Paul's purpose is actually very anthropological: the parallel sheds light on human nature with and without Jesus. In this regard, the idea of freedom is arguably the most pervasive and most characteristic feature of the human being who has been transformed by incorporation into the dying and rising of Jesus.

Paul was acutely sensitive to the liberating effect of the death of Jesus. One becomes aware of this whenever Paul begins speaking about the Law. Paul articulates his grasp of the grace of God as liberating against the background of his own religious and cultural roots, which is understandable. Yet it is, perhaps, unfortunate that Paul never knew the historical Jesus sufficiently to be able to draw firsthand upon examples of Jesus' own freedom. There is no doubt that behind Paul's encounter with the risen Jesus lies a profound realization of being set free, a realization which would require time before coming fully into consciousness. Furthermore, Paul worked this notion of freedom out in such a way as to make it possible for the church to transcend the religious and cultural limitations imposed by its Jewish roots, as James Dunn points out in his commentary on the letter to the Romans (*Romans 1–8* [Dallas: Word Books, 1988], p. xvi). Such a step had to be taken. Otherwise, what interest would those outside of Israel—the Greeks, the Romans, the Egyptians, just to name a few—have had in the fortunes of a failed prophet and crucified "savior" from a remote area of Palestine? The message of freedom and liberation had to be pitched in a key they could hear, too.

Yet if Paul were alive today, it would be natural enough to expect that he would have worked through his understanding of Christian freedom in very different terms. For today, the areas where human beings most acutely confront sin, slavery and death are injustice, poverty and the suppression of human rights. Such things were not on Paul's mind when he wrote the thirteenth chapter of his letter to the Romans. Such spiritual counsel to oppressed and impoverished people in a world which has awakened to democratic ideals would be fundamentally contrary to the gospel Paul had received. If Paul had considered at length the confrontations Jesus engaged in with the religious and political authorities of his day, then his advice to the Christian communities in Rome might have been framed somewhat differently. In context, Paul's remarks might have been most prudent. Today, they could be read as lending support to governments which rule by terror and intimidation. Paul's words

> This is why you also pay taxes, for the authorities are ministers of God, devoting themselves to this very thing. Pay to all their dues, taxes to whom taxes are due, toll to whom toll is due . . . (Rom 13:6–7)

make sound practical advice for individuals struggling to survive in a hostile religious and political environment. But could they be the sentiments of Jesus? And if some of those taxes were going to be used to support the imperial army in its bloody repression of political and religious freedom in his own beloved Israel, would Paul in conscience have been able to deliver the same instruction?

There is a good reason to raise these points in a discussion about the resurrection. The apostle Paul had certainly grasped the idea that a brand-new type of existence had been inaugurated with the resurrection of Jesus. It was as if a new human being had been created, a second Adam. This fresh possibility for being human represented a significant intervention of God within human history, on a par with the great events of the Old Testament. But the transformation of the human involved more than a transposition to a new symbolic key. Something new had happened within history which could drastically affect the shape of the future of that history, and of every individual's future within it. The symbols were illuminating, but they had to be related to the concrete circumstances of everyday lives. And at the level of the concrete, within his own person, Paul had internalized and understood the freedom of the children of God. It was that freedom which Jesus had exhibited all through his ministry, the freedom which characterized him as God's beloved Son and which established the pattern for the story of our being set free, too. In other words, the freedom which Paul had discovered as a result of his encounter with the risen Jesus was the very freedom which characterized Jesus himself all through his life.

In light of Paul's insight, the question we need to address to ourselves might well be, "Do I want to be truly free, the way Jesus was?" There is something wonderfully wholesome about a person fully free, provided that freedom springs from the Spirit and has been learned from Jesus. For genuine freedom is not achieved when one makes freedom itself the goal; personal moral (or spiritual) perfection is not the goal of being-with-Jesus. The goal, rather, is being-for-others in the mode of someone who has learned the lessons about the kingdom of God.

35

People of Little Faith

On a variety of occasions throughout the gospel story, Jesus expressed amazement over people's lack of faith and, what is often associated with this, their hardness of heart. When the townsfolk of Nazareth rejected Jesus, he expressed amazement over their unwillingness to believe (Mk 6:6). Mark tells us that the reason the disciples did not recognize Jesus walking toward them on the water was that their hearts were hardened (Mk 6:52), which is precisely the question Jesus asked them after they misunderstood his allusion to the leaven of the Pharisees and of Herod, and fell into arguing about some bread: "Are your hearts hardened?" (Mk 8:17)

In the so-called longer ending to Mark's gospel we read that the risen Jesus reprimanded the disciples for their unbelief and hardness of heart, since they had not accepted the testimony of the first Easter witnesses (Mk 16:14). Matthew had added to Mark's story of the walking on the water an incident about Peter's attempting to walk toward Jesus over the lake, too. Peter became frightened and started to sink. On that occasion Jesus said, "O you of little faith, why did you doubt?" (Mt 15:31) And later, on the mount of the ascension, the disciples were still doubting, presumably about the identity of the risen Jesus (Mt 28:17). Throughout the fourth gospel, Jesus repeatedly accuses people of not having faith, that is, of not truly knowing God. If they did, then they would certainly have recognized Jesus as the one sent by the Father.

Why Faith?

Jesus' insistence upon faith leads us to ask what precisely he was calling (or expecting) people to believe in. In the case of the miracles, it is clear that he was asking people to believe in the power of God, just as he himself did. If Jesus had not been a believer himself, then it would have been unfair of him to expect faith of others. His words to the father of the epileptic boy would have been hollow (Mk 9:23).

Yet having a faith that issued in miracles did not exhaust what it meant to be a believer. To say that Jesus above all was summoning men and women to repentance does not tell us enough, since there would have been other voices inviting the people to this; repentance is a pervasive religious theme. No matter how bleak we presume the state of people's spiritual lives at the time of Jesus to be (for why else would God send Jesus among us?), we have to admit that at least some people were reading and listening to the prophetic voices of old, and repenting; many were disposed to amending their lives. Otherwise, one could never account for the response of so many people to the preaching of John. Yet to say that Jesus was inviting people to put their faith in him goes too far. That would come later, especially in John's gospel, for the fourth evangelist realized that life in the Spirit involved faith in Jesus risen, who was the sacrament of the kingdom (and presence) of God. The fact is that we are so used to visualizing Jesus calling people to faith that we probably never determined what exactly he was expecting of them.

Wasn't it natural for people to have some doubts? Why should anyone have believed, before the resurrection, that this man was indeed God's Anointed, the great Prophet? On the basis of miracles? And given the extraordinary nature of the claim that someone had actually been raised from the dead, why should anyone be "amazed" that people did not readily and automatically accept this news? What led Jesus to think that because he was so enthusiastic about the kingdom of God, everyone else would share his enthusiasm? Jesus may have been utterly charismatic, but charism alone could not usher in the kingdom; only God could do that. Or are the questions about lack of faith nothing more than story-telling devices to bring readers into the narrative and elicit their faith response? In other words, are the incidents about the disciples' lack of faith and hardness of heart actually placed in the gospel narrative for our benefit? I suspect that this is largely what has happened. The fact that the disciples of Jesus are frequently rebuked for their lack of faith pressures us, the readers, not to succumb to the same thing.

For his part, Jesus was proclaiming that the great promise of God was about to be fulfilled; the hopes of people, especially the hopes of poor people, were at last going to be realized. And he was asking others to put their faith in this, which amounted to asking them to trust his experience of God. It would be unfair to suggest that everyone who failed to respond to Jesus was guilty of hardness of heart, although it is interesting to observe that in many instances those who did accept Jesus' message were men and women who had experienced God's forgiveness and compassion. Sinners appeared to be in a more advantageous position for hearing the good news which Jesus preached than the righteous. One's willingness to trust the divine promise was correlative to the vitality of one's hopes and desires, and hope is much more pronounced among the poor, the oppressed, the outcast, and the sinners.

For Jesus, faith meant relinquishing one's self and one's future, unconditionally, into the hands of God, no matter where that might take us. This was the faith of Abraham, Isaac, Jacob and their descendants; this was the faith of David, Elijah, and each of the prophets. It is the meaning of faith, too, for all truly righteous men and women throughout history. But while the act of faith itself would be the same for all men and women, the particular conditions which frame that faith are not. Thus, for Jesus, his faith was conditioned by Israel's longstanding hope for liberation and freedom: the inauguration of the messianic age in the present, and for the future, God's ultimate deliverance of the whole world. Jesus' own faith directed him to preach to the poor, to the defenseless, to those burdened by guilt, and to those whom society had cast away.

Faith Confers a Sense of Urgency

Probably like many other people my age, I grew accustomed over the years to hearing the Beatitudes uttered calmly, soothingly and reassuringly, and as a result that was how I always imagined Jesus to have delivered them. As I grow older, however, I have begun to think that Jesus delivered the Beatitudes with anger in his voice; they were protests against the status quo. He was exasperated and irate because the secure, the well-to-do and the righteous had no felt need for God, like the Pharisee who was unable to understand the gift of forgiveness because he never visualized himself in the position of truly needing it (Lk 7:44–47).

"Blessed are you who are poor," Jesus said, "for the kingdom of God is yours" (Lk 6:20). Instead of imagining a kind and gentle Jesus speaking these words, suppose we were to hear these words spoken with angry, almost thunderous tones, as a prophet might utter them. Jesus would be supporting the poor, not with the gentle reassurance of future reward, but with a forceful, impassioned guarantee that they will inherit the divine promise. Outraged over their poverty (and the conditions which have made them poor), Jesus practically cries, "Blessed are you!" His mood is one of defiance. The accent of the beatitude falls on the second part: it is the poor who will receive the kingdom; they can count on God for that! What warrants our reading the text this way is the occurrence of "But woe to you" in the ensuing verses. Those are not soft words, patiently cautioning the wealthy to be more considerate of the less fortunate, but bold denunciations. Jesus' prophetic anger could not be clearer. It is only matched in intensity by the denunciations of the scribes and Pharisees in Matthew 23.

The reason for recalling the anger of Jesus is that this can help us to appreciate how utterly convinced he was of the message he had been preaching. He had taken the promise of God with the utmost seriousness, while many others had not. When he marvels at their lack of belief, are we to conclude that the people to whom he speaks are godless and totally without faith? Or is it that they have forgotten that the God of Israel is a God who acts? Are they people who keep looking forward to deliverance, but then, when the opportunity is presented to them, take refuge in the "real" world: a world where everything has its prescribed or accustomed place, including God? Has God become nothing more than a symbol of the past, remembered for once having done great wonders, but whom no one seriously expects to change things? Besides, consider all the failed prophets and messianic pretenders. What would have led people to believe that things would be any different with Jesus? Indeed, wasn't Jesus being harsh to reprimand his followers for not believing him, or for not readily accepting the testimony of hysterical women who were reporting that he had been raised from the dead?

The choice before us is whether to be believers as Jesus was a believer, or not. Are we prepared to let our experience of God be based on his? Are we ready to let our act of faith be shaped by the God of Israel, the Creator-God who acts in history, who liberates, who makes promises, and who even raises the dead to life? To accept the resurrection is to do much more than give notional assent to the proposition that God raised Jesus from the dead. For behind the resurrection lies the question, What sort of God does such things? What was God protesting? Why was it so important that Jesus remain in the world, animating and leading his brothers and sisters, through the power of the Spirit? The answer is that the kingdom of God—the kingdom of promise—was at hand. And still is.

What is at stake is the possibility of concretely realizing what Jesus envisioned by the kingdom of God even here and now. The kingdom is not just an "eschatological" reality, that is, something which will make complete sense only against the horizon of God's fulfilled desires or plans for the human race. However incomplete its realization, the kingdom of God is offered to us even now, before the end of history. After all, one cannot automatically assume that by the end of time, "all manner of things will be well." One can hope for this, but it would be naive to believe that the human race in its entirety will someday finally accept God's offer of redemption. Nevertheless, the resurrection of Jesus urges us forward by saying, "Let us start!" Jesus' impatience over his followers' slowness to believe and their hardness of heart is the impatience of one who knows what the future can be. What appears to have exasperated him is our reluctance to step onto the waves, even when he is clearly in sight, standing reassuringly ahead of us, and to trust the impossible.

36

A Day in the Life

The first chapter of Mark presents what might be described as a typical day in the life of Jesus early in his public ministry. The activity apparently lasted late into the night. Early the next day, before the sun had risen, Mark tells us, Jesus went off to a deserted place to pray. Perhaps the previous day's activity had drained his spirit and he was feeling the need to be back in touch with the experience of God which marked his stay in the wilderness. In the future he would seek out lonely and deserted places, almost as if that foundational experience of God in the wilderness needed to be retrieved from time to time. At any rate, Peter and the other companions went out looking for Jesus. Upon locating him they said, "Everyone is looking for you" (Mk 1:37). One can easily imagine the disciples being somewhat frustrated. Jesus had become the center of attention; crowds had begun flocking to him, people were becoming enthusiastic, expectations were being raised, and Jesus appears to have fled! Then instead of returning to Capernaum and capitalizing on the spectacular beginning he had made, Jesus tells his companions, "Let us go to the nearby villages that I may preach there also" (1:38).

In his book *The Historical Jesus*, John Dominic Crossan raised the intriguing possibility that the reason Jesus decided to leave Capernaum was to prevent Peter and the others from thinking that they could "broker" (to use Crossan's word) the kingdom of God. For, all of a sudden, Peter's home had become very important. In the Galilean peasant society of the time, this unexpected notoriety would have fed the desire of Peter and his friends to be important, even to be the agents who would admit the sick and infirm into the presence of Jesus the healer. Similarly, the reason why the peasants of Nazareth were so upset with Jesus, Crossan continues, is that Jesus would not allow them to become "brokers" of the kingdom, either. Their petulant request that he work the same wonders in Nazareth which he had in Capernaum (Lk 4:23) betrays the same attitude: people wanted to get in on the act; they wanted to reap something from the fallout surrounding Jesus' display of power. In short, what was surfacing was the same attitude we would observe on the road to Jerusalem: people were thinking about power, while Jesus was thinking about service.

I am not satisfied that Crossan's suggestion accounts for Jesus' decision to begin journeying to the other villages, but it certainly corresponds to what Mark tells us about the disciples thinking as human beings do, and not as God does. To me it makes better sense to propose that, at least at this early stage, it was out of excitement that Jesus turned to the surrounding towns and hamlets. The response which had greeted him in Capernaum would naturally lead him to want to spread the good news more widely. Moreover, he would soon be returning to Capernaum, and, we would presume, to Peter's home (2:1). Crossan's point is, nevertheless, well taken. Jesus' sense of how the dynamics of the kingdom worked was not at all pragmatic according to the world's standards. He himself had already confronted the issues of power versus service, honor versus shame, wealth versus poverty (or freedom), being well-connected versus being marginalized, and so forth; such were the lessons from his struggle in the wilderness. Yet after a while the disciples would understand: it was the resurrection that finally opened their minds to how God worked.

In chapter 6, Mark reports that Jesus was once again moving around the villages and teaching. On that occasion, he also sent out the disciples in what sounds like a great exercise for developing a lived dependence upon God. They apparently went from house to house, and stayed wherever they found themselves welcomed. Their strategy might have been to begin conversing about the kingdom of God with the welcoming family and their neighbors, just the way Jesus had been doing at Peter's house in Capernaum. The enthusiasm of Jesus was spreading around the countryside through his companions. Interestingly, between the missioning of the disciples and their return, Mark sandwiches the story about the beheading of John the Baptist, suggesting, maybe, that for messengers of God such a fate is always lurking in the background. Needless to say, the disciples themselves had to have been aware of the sobering news about John. However buoyant their spirits felt, they would also have had to live with the prospect that they likewise could be arrested and put to death.

Furthermore, if the pattern of missionary activity after the resurrection in any way reflects the pattern of mission work during Jesus' lifetime, then Paul's question in his correspondence with the Christians at Corinth suggests an interesting possibility: "Do we not have the right to take along a Christian wife, as do the rest of the apostles, and the brothers of the Lord, and Kephas?" (1 Cor 9:5) While Mark records that Jesus sent the Twelve out "two by two," this would not preclude some of them being accompanied by their wives, or an older son. In fact, the idea that some of them might have embarked on their preaching tour as couples would only underscore further the radical freedom of Jesus and the fundamental equality of men and women in the kingdom of God. (And Paul's reference to Jesus' brothers implies, if we read between the lines, that Jesus was most likely an uncle.)

My reason for bringing up these points is simply to tease the imagination. The story of Jesus, insofar as possible, should be humanly proportioned. While the gospels occasionally recount some fantastic elements within the story, by and large it can be read as having taken place within a world to which we, too, can relate. What happened in the lives of Peter and his family, or the other companions, or Mary of Magdala, or the relatives of Jesus, or close friends of Jesus like Martha, Mary and their brother Lazarus, could equally as well have happened to us. All of them were plain, ordinary people. All of them led lives which included many of the same tensions, joys, activities and rituals which mark our lives. When Jesus broke into their worlds, eager, joyous, sincere and radiant with hope, nothing would ever be the same again.

The fact that Jesus healed and "expelled demons" need not make our picture of him any less real or less human. The fact is that people were coming to meet him, to listen to him, to share with him their own insight and hope. Apart from the demon-possessed (who form a special case), the gospels do not record anyone who ran away from Jesus. To be sure, as his reputation grew, Jesus assumed some celebrity status. Yet he never became unapproachable, and when the disciples tried to shoo away the mothers who were bringing their small children to him, Jesus corrected them (Mk 10:13). One time, at home in Capernaum, the disciples had to confess to Jesus about arguing with one another over who among them was the greatest (Mk 9:33). He then took a little child, first had him stand in the middle of the room, and then grabbed him in his arms. Children, of course, were both defenseless and (at least in the minds of the disciples) of little use in preaching such wonderful ideas as the kingdom of God.

Jesus directs the attention of his companions once again to the simple, plain reality in front of them and says, "Whoever receives one child such as this in my name, receives me" (9:37). So much for being an apostle! Even a child can represent Jesus! The problem here, as on many other occasions, is that the companions have become so caught up in what they think the kingdom of God is about that they neglect what is closest to home. But what draws our attention about the scene is that the child's presence is simply taken for granted. In other words, there were probably children around the house, maybe Peter's, maybe some belonging to a few of the other disciples. Again, it is the ordinariness of things that the imagination needs to dwell on. People would come to listen and to converse, others would bring along their infirm relatives and friends to be healed, and sometimes perhaps even "important" people dropped by to speak with Jesus. And amidst all of this, kids were running in and out of the house.

It is not altogether clear what things were like when Jesus and his companions were on the road together. Yet even there, if it is permitted to read between the lines, they must have made contact with families. Friends and relatives back home might know people elsewhere where they could find lodging, one contact would lead to another, and once more they probably found themselves in the middle of domestic scenes not unlike their own. Sharing meals, eating whatever families out of their goodness and their means might offer, they would enter into conversation about the approaching kingdom of God. Repentance and forgiveness, the basic equality all enjoyed because all were daughters and sons of the same Father, the common struggle for justice against those who lorded over the poor and defenseless, shared disappointment over the state of official religious leadership, the need to transcend prejudices, the healing closeness of God, the risk of faith: these must have been some of the familiar themes which could engage people endlessly, until the early hours of the morning. The same thing might repeat itself the next day. And once the fire was kindled, the companions would move on to the next village.

I do not picture Jesus fraternizing with hardened criminals; the two would not have had any more in common at that time than they would today. Indeed, Jesus sought out sinners, and they sought him out, too. But I have trouble trying to picture Jesus, were he alive now, engaging, say, hard-core drug dealers. However, I do know of people who have turned to stealing, even to pushing some small-time contraband, because they lack any social resources to survive otherwise. I have known poor people to cash a dead relative's welfare checks. Lives sometimes get very hard and opportunities to make a decent living extremely scarce. I have seen young people treated as non-persons, threatened and intimidated by the police, for no other reason than that they "look" suspicious. But their only crime is that they are Hispanic, or black. If these are the gospel's "sinners," then it is easy to imagine Jesus among them, and feeling comfortable.

Maybe this is what makes the parable of the rich man who had problems with a dishonest manager so charming (Lk 16:1–8). The manager, or steward, was basically a crook; but he was also a survivor. Jesus must have warmed to him, because the parable concludes, "And the master commended that dishonest steward for acting prudently" (Lk 16:8). But what is more to the point, the parable is informing us that Jesus must have been aware of such behavior; and if Jesus was aware, so was everyone else. Dishonesty was simply a part of life, especially where people were forced to survive by their wits at society's edge. The fact that the Son of God should have been crucified between two crooks contains a marvelous divine irony. Jesus was found with them in death, just as he had been at home with them during his life. The prostitutes and tax-collectors, after all, were not the only professional sinners.

For the most part, the life of Jesus was ordinary. I do not mean that he was *just* another person; far from it! Rather, he was the sort of person whose presence radically challenges and changes the way everyone else views the world. The gospel parables were continually tipping the familiar world on its edge, which tells us that this is exactly what Jesus himself was doing, not just by his words, but by his actions and his presence. Mark seems to have had some fascination with demons, because they keep popping out of scenes, threatening to disclose Jesus' great secret. Yet, in the end, there really was no secret: "For there is nothing hidden except to be made visible; nothing is secret except to come to light" (Mk 4:22). In the end, Jesus was recognized to be the Son of God. The demons may have been Mark's technique of imposing, like some transparency, a background drama upon the story of

Jesus in which the great contest taking place was pitched between the powers of good and evil. The life of Jesus may have appeared ordinary, but what was really going on had cosmic dimensions; the kingdom of God was opposed to every counter-kingdom. And anyone who could not see the difference between the two kingdoms, between Jesus and the prince of demons, could be guilty of an everlasting sin (Mk 3:29). The intrusion of the demons, like the transfiguration, alerts the reader to the truth that more is going on than meets the eye. Yet that is the way things always are, even amidst the ordinariness of our lives, too.

37

Two Summary Points

As we start to draw to the end of this material, I would like to ask you, the reader, two questions: What features of the story of Jesus would you stress if you were telling it, and what makes Jesus unique? When I posed these questions to my own students, five points kept emerging under one form or another. They would emphasize (1) Jesus' humanity, (2) his openness to people, (3) his relationship with God, (4) his oneness with the poor, and (5) the social dimensions of his message. I was gratified that they had picked up on these features, since they are all based on the gospel texts we have been looking at rather than on preconceived notions of what being God's Son might have meant. In response to the question about what makes Jesus unique they proposed (1) his being raised from the dead, since that cannot be claimed of anyone else in history, and (2) his selflessness, which they would measure in terms of the brutality of the death he willingly underwent.

It should be pointed out that, while the resurrection is truly distinctive, it might be presumptuous to say that Jesus' death was more horrible than anyone else's, or that his selflessness could be singled out as being greater than that of any other person. Whenever human beings give totally of themselves, then their selflessness is complete; there is nothing more to give. Measured in human terms, Jesus' love would have been as great as any human love could be, but the same could be said of many other people, too, who have loved with all their heart, soul, mind and strength. His capability for loving was the human capability. If Jesus surmounted limitations so that he loved to the fullness of his God-given capability, then, theoretically at least, other human beings could do the same. In fact, we call them saints.

While the above points are important, there are two additional ones which deserve to be doubly underlined. First, *the forgiveness of sins* played a prominent role in Jesus' ministry, so much so that the gospel tradition preserves the memory of his dying in order that sins might be forgiven. This feature should be included in any version of the gospel story. The forgiveness of sins was the gospel's favorite code for expressing the entire range of full human liberation, God's setting men and women free from everything which interfered with, compromised or damaged their integrity and freedom as God's children. And secondly, the source of Jesus' action and teaching in terms of what both enlightened him and empowered him was *his experience of God*. This puts things a little more sharply than simply saying that Jesus enjoyed a special relationship with God. This relationship was a function of his experience. Jesus could be called "Son" because he experienced God as "Father." Experiencing God as Father, Jesus lived and taught accordingly. And what is of the greatest importance as far as we are concerned is that this "special" relationship was not exclusive; other men and women could share it, because of Jesus.

This realization is what lies at the basis of the church's later trinitarian formulation of faith. Whatever conceptual terminology is invoked in order to explain this, the simple fact is that the disciples of Jesus found themselves living at the base of an experience, as James Dunn explains in *Jesus and the Spirit*. They experienced Jesus to be still present among them. They also found themselves relating to God in a manner very different from the way they would have related to God before ever encountering Jesus. They further discovered that Jesus could never be bracketed out of this experience: being-with-Jesus was the only route to their experience of the God that Jesus knew. Finally, what made this relationship come alive was the Spirit, or to be precise, the Spirit of Jesus.

38

Acting with the Spirit of Jesus

At the very beginning I proposed two questions to guide us as we walked through the story of Jesus: Who is Jesus? What would I be willing to do together with him? The answer to the first question most likely is going to get formulated in the process of talking about him. One reads the gospels. One listens to one's own experience of life and of the world. One seeks out other men and women for whom this question is also important, and one begins to speak about the things of faith. Above all, one gets inside the story, because the story itself holds enormous power to draw us into the world of the gospel where men and women first met and walked with Jesus. Then, on the basis of one's developing or clarifying idea of who Jesus is, one soon discovers that life is not the same anymore.

As the character of Jesus becomes more human and the person of Jesus becomes more tangible, and even before we have settled on adequately descriptive titles for him, we are going to find ourselves pulled increasingly into noticing what Jesus does, the human manner in which he may have done it, and the reaction of the various characters or groups around him. What becomes more and more attractive and desirable about him is the wholesomeness of his humanity: his freedom, his compassion, his integrity, his readiness to see and speak the truth, his deep affection for other men and women, his God-centeredness. Gradually we awaken to how earnestly we want the same wholeness for ourselves, and we do not feel at all selfish about wanting it. For in this case, we are being instinctively drawn toward someone fully alive, which is the most natural and healthy thing in the world for us to do. In the presence of Jesus, whom the evangelists call the Son of

God, we notice ourselves wanting above all to be like him; in this lies our salvation or liberation.

Who Then Is Jesus?

While each of us might wind up answering this question a little differently, the gospels themselves offer a wide selection of possibilities. Jesus is the Messiah or Savior, the Christ or Anointed One; Jesus is the teacher, healer and companion who is Wisdom itself and Compassion or Love itself. Jesus is the Prophet of the kingdom, the Lord, or even the model of true service. He is the friend of sinners and outcasts. Jesus is God's own beloved Son, the one who has enabled us to experience God in a way both unique and wonderfully satisfying. Or, following the lead of the fourth gospel, Jesus is the way, the truth and the life (Jn 14:6). "Way," "truth" and "life" are interconnected, experiential categories, for they shed light on what men and women actually experience when they encounter Jesus and spend time in his company. Who, finally, is Jesus? This is going to depend upon what our experience of him has been. An institutionally supplied answer, apart from any underlying relationship with him, is going to sound hollow, and it will be simply incapable of providing sufficient energy for the individual to give radical Christian witness. Why, after all, would a person attempt anything truly radical or revolutionary? Why dare the obviously foolish step of trying to walk over the waves? The only thing that would make such risk possible is the desire to be with Jesus, and to be doing things the way he did.

As we review the story of Jesus, some scenes are going to stand out more prominently than others. Mark portrays Jesus as healing and teaching, always pointing men and women toward the kingdom of God. The signs and miracles of Jesus are essentially signs of the kingdom. The manner and the content of his teaching were meant to enable his listeners to view the world as God views it, which is the essence of all contemplative prayer. Liberation names the action of God within human history, and therefore justice emerges as one of the preeminent virtues of the kingdom. The other virtue is compassion, and behind both of them stands the mystery of God, which is love.

What Am I Prepared to Do Together with Jesus?

To answer this question requires that we have first learned what sorts of things Jesus himself did. That is why it is so important to steep our imaginations in the gospel story. As we have seen, many of the things Jesus did were truly prophetic in character. They had to be, because Jesus' call to repent and believe in the gospel was predicated on the biblical insight that links the action of believing with doing justice. Isaiah had said:

> Make justice your aim: redress the wronged,
> hear the orphan's plea, defend the widow. (Isa 1:17)

and again:

> For the Lord is a God of justice. (Isa 30:18)

Now, how could a person be truly believing, unless he or she was prepared to do whatever God required? How could someone have a faith-relationship with the God of Israel, unless he or she was prepared to share God's concerns? There is nothing that the disciples of Jesus would be expected to do which Jesus himself has not first done; and there is nothing which the disciples of Jesus would be expected to do alone: Jesus would always be with them in the Spirit, and "in the Spirit" they could truthfully and honestly imagine themselves in his company. Imagination helps us to visualize our being-with-Jesus in the Spirit.

To act with the Spirit of Jesus means, first of all, that one acts as Jesus himself would act. Through the gospel story, it becomes possible for men and women in every generation to internalize the mind and heart of Jesus, just as his first companions did. But to act with the Spirit of Jesus also means something else. It also means that one is living and acting *with* Jesus *in* the Spirit. The Christian does not live alone. Whenever the Christian acts "in the Spirit," Jesus is acting with us, and in us, and through us; he becomes really and powerfully present in the world through the lives of his disciples. But I do not want to wax theological and abstract; I prefer to let imagination do the work. Just as it is possible, through the gospel story, for us to be there with him; so too it is possible for him, through the same story, to be here with us.

What Happened to the Kingdom?

Finally, what about the kingdom of God? One of my favorite ways of priming a discussion is to ask, "If Jesus were among us today, in person, what would he be doing? Where would we find him?" Such questions force us to clarify our images of Jesus and probe our knowledge of the gospels. What was foremost for Jesus was the kingdom of God, a reality which he clearly envisioned as imminent and which would also be founded upon a particular experience of the God of Israel.

Yet despite the signs and the parables, somehow we have a difficult time imagining exactly what the kingdom was supposed to be like. We are so accustomed to straddling the distinction between the kingdom and heaven, that it is easy to slip into identifying the kingdom as everlasting life, or life in "the world to come." For Jesus, however, the kingdom was God's offer of something brand-new here and now; heaven will be too late for those who are thirsting for justice, because they suffer now. The great liberation has to start here; otherwise, it is both useless and foolish to continue to trust the great promise of God. For Jesus, the oppressed are not going to leave the earth; they are going to inherit it. The kingdom is that great promise, but its realization depends upon human response. Again we ask, "What am I prepared to do with Jesus?"

Although the gospel's picture of the kingdom (which seems to oscillate between the present and the future, as something which has begun and at the same time as something yet to come) may not be altogether clear, nevertheless its picture of Jesus' experience of God (however incomplete) is far clearer: God is absolutely close, compassionate, and preferentially in love with those at the bottom of society; God is absolutely trustworthy and intolerant of every form of injustice and oppression; God heals, loves, reconciles and liberates; God breaks down the barriers that keep human beings apart.

For the person whose experience of God is forever inseparable from being-with-Jesus, there is both a mission and a goal. The "what" or the object of what we are prepared to do is nothing less than to continue working, in and with the Spirit of Jesus, for the very same things that Jesus did. One increasingly shares Jesus' social sensitivity and prophetic insight: his compassion and his politics, as it were. More and more, one notices alienation and estrangement, and the scandalous contradiction between belief and practice. One's values become the values of the kingdom, as one is impressed less and less with power, prestige and wealth. Justice becomes one's goal, which demands a conversion and purification of soul so that one continually views life through the eyes of those on the bottom. One's attitude toward family and friends undergoes a change, as one's understanding of what constitutes true family grows. One perceives how God is at home in ordinary human realities and the hustle of daily life. One is no longer intimidated by what others think, or by what they might be able to do to harm or defeat us; one begins to dare to speak the truth, confidently and boldly.

That God is definitively and irrevocably on the side of those who are peacemakers, who show mercy, who hunger and thirst for righteousness, who are poor in spirit, is forcefully revealed by the resurrection of Jesus. God did not, and will never, allow his faithful ones to undergo corruption: neither their efforts, nor their hopes, nor their very selves. Imagine Jesus praying the Psalm:

> I set the Lord ever before me;
>   with him at my right hand I shall not be disturbed.
> Therefore my heart is glad and my soul rejoices,
>   my body, too, abides in confidence;
> Because you will not abandon my soul to the nether world,
>   nor will you suffer your faithful one to undergo corruption.
>   (Ps 16:8–11)

These verses, which the early church applied to the raising of Jesus from the dead, apply equally well to the experience of those who are his disciples and companions. For those who dedicate themselves to living the gospel, and who both hope and work for that transfigured reality which will be humanity made new, the story of Jesus is itself both the parable and the paradigm of life in the kingdom of God. The story of Jesus has been sown in our imaginations. Even as we speak, that seed is already sprouting and growing, day by day, although we have no idea how (Mk 4:26–28).

Epilogue

While all the episodes of *Un tal Jesus* are skillfully and imaginatively drawn, two of them are particularly effective. The first is the re-telling of the story of the lost sheep. Within the book, the context is Jesus' just having made Matthew's acquaintance and accepted an invitation to dinner at his house. The disciples are absolutely dismayed. Zebedee, the father of James and John, is so enraged at Jesus' having dealings with tax-collector scum like Matthew that he warns him, once he crosses into Matthew's home, that he will never again be welcome back in his house. Later, Jesus is seated at Capernaum's equivalent of a tavern and speaking with the others, who are still very much upset with him; the disciples and Jesus had just had their first big argument. As usual, Jesus takes the occasion to recount a story he remembers from his childhood about a shepherd tending a hundred sheep. One of the flock, we learn, is slower than the rest because it is lame. As the story unfolds, the shepherd is distraught when he cannot locate his one-hundredth sheep. It is growing late. A storm is brewing. The howling of wolves can be heard in the hills. The action moves back and forth between the sad cries of the lost sheep and the thoughts of the shepherd. The other shepherds urge him not to worry, reminding him that the lame sheep had always been a bother anyway and a constant source of anxiety. He would be better off abandoning it to the wolves. As the shepherd bundles himself under his warm blankets, he decides, finally, that the other shepherds are right, and he falls off to sleep. Meanwhile, the lost sheep can be heard wailing, having stumbled down a steep hill into a pond, where it drowns.

All at once the disciples begin shouting at Jesus and arguing. They don't like the story. They are furious at the behavior of the shepherd who takes his sleep in comfort as the poor lost sheep cries in the wilderness.

214

But, says Jesus, sipping his wine, that is the ending which the disciples themselves wanted! They are dumbfounded and ask what in the world he means, and Jesus answers that such is the way they have treated Matthew. "Fortunately," Jesus goes on to say, "God has written a different ending." He then proceeds to tell the familiar version.

The second episode is the story of Peter's walking on the sea and nearly drowning. The story is being recounted to us when, at the very point where Peter begins gulping water and shouting to Jesus, "Save me, I'm drowning!" his wife starts to shake him awake. The action on the lake was all a dream! But as Peter finishes telling his wife about the dream, he starts exclaiming, like someone who has just stumbled upon a marvelous piece of news, "He is the One!" "What one?" she asks. Peter answers, "The Messiah!" Then the narrator breaks in (who, throughout the whole account, is John, the son of Zebedee) and says that years later, as Peter recalled that night, he was still unable to determine whether the scene on the water had really happened, or whether it was just a dream. Yet the one thing of which Peter was absolutely convinced from that moment was that Jesus was indeed the One who was to come.

What I find so skillful about these reconstructions is the way they intensify the effect of the stories. In the first case, it is the failure of the shepherd to spend himself for his lost sheep that prepares us to hear the wonderful news about the way God would write the story's ending. Otherwise, one could easily take the point of the story as it is normally told for granted: God is the good shepherd; so what else would we expect? Indeed, God may be; but human beings may not be, and it is because human beings often prove so untrustworthy and uncompassionate that the weak, defenseless and poor ones among us perish. It goes without saying that this is not what the gospel literally says, but the dramatic effect has been rendered much stronger. Viewers of the film *Jesus of Nazareth* may recall that Zeffirelli did something similar when he juxtaposed Jesus' encounter with Levi (and the subsequent supper in Levi's house) with Jesus' telling the story of the prodigal son, while Peter, who has refused to go inside, listens from the doorway. The effect was quite moving as Peter came to the realization that he had been behaving like the elder brother.

The second episode grabs our attention because the story of Peter's walking on the lake already strikes many readers as unreal and made-up. Precisely because it sounds fictitious, we tell ourselves, the story must have a symbolic meaning; the lesson has to be that we must trust Jesus to the limit. In the Latin American retelling, however, the fact that the whole sequence occurs in a dream actually makes the story more real.

On the basis of the little we have seen from Mark's gospel, the proclamation (in Matthew's gospel) of the disciples in the boat, "Truly, you are the Son of God," coupled with their doing him homage (Mt 14:33), appears premature. Such certitude about the identity of Jesus almost certainly came some time after Easter. Yet if the point of the story is to elicit a faith-response from the reader, then we can more easily relate to Peter's insight into Jesus through a dream than through such a miraculous feat. It would be unfortunate if we allowed our natural reticence to accept the miracle prevent us from seconding the disciples' affirmation, "Truly, you are the Son of God." Actually, the real point here is not so much about the personal identity of Jesus; it is not even about the disciples' recognition of that identity. Rather, the real point is about what they are prepared to do: would they be willing to step foot onto a stormy sea if they saw Jesus beckoning them to come? Would they do such a thing because they trusted him?

Anyone who has taken a grave risk, precisely as a response to the call of the Spirit, or in the effort to follow Jesus, comprehends the meaning of this scene. To inform readers puzzled by the miracle that the story is the fruit of Easter faith and insight does not get their imaginations off the hook. Miracle or no miracle, what would we do if we were in Peter's position? In this case, as in so many others, our faith is ultimately going to rest on the faith of the disciples. Consequently, we are supposed to be responding not to the supernatural feat but to the faith out of which Mark narrates this story about Jesus. We glimpse the faith that got Peter to dare to approach Jesus over the waves, and we feel the lack of faith that nearly caused this great fisherman to drown. What confirms our faith is not going to be a miracle, but the experience of taking a risk in response to the Spirit of Jesus. Walking over the waves is the gospel's way of picturing radical Christian witness.

How Shall We Talk about Jesus Today?

As I see it, the way to talk about Jesus today requires that we do more than simply repeat the gospel accounts of Jesus' life and ministry.

It also calls for creative retelling of the gospel story in ways that put people in touch with the faith of the communities which composed the gospels, as well as of those communities which have handed them down to us over the centuries. Of course, such retelling cannot bypass sound biblical and historical scholarship; but, as always, scholarship serves faith. It also serves imagination, for it is through imagination that the world of the gospel is re-created.

In addition, talking about Jesus today always presupposes that Jesus is real for the storyteller. And if Jesus is real, then in some mysterious way his story is also unfolding today. It unfolds in the life of the storyteller himself or herself, and it unfolds in the life of the believing community. We cannot talk about Jesus, therefore, without revealing ourselves at the same time. The gospel has a knack of bringing what is secret or hidden into the open. Whoever lights a lamp intends that people should see; whoever starts to tell the story of Jesus is lighting a lamp within his own soul, so that what one is becomes translucent. Whenever sin sets in the human heart, it becomes impossible honestly to tell people about Jesus; one's own life no longer corresponds to the story one is endeavoring to narrate. That is true of us as individuals, and it holds true for the church itself.

Although the answer might seem to be embarrassingly obvious, we do need to ask why telling the story of Jesus today remains so important. In the last few years, the church has been addressing itself to the task of evangelization, since there appears to have been some failure on the part of the Catholic community to speak its message, boldly and persuasively, to the non-believing world. The vitality of the community's faith, it has often been suggested, can be measured in terms of its missionary spirit. Today, Catholics seem to be timid, reluctant, even apathetic about sharing their faith with outsiders; they appear to be content with collaboration, with a commitment to common humanitarian goals, and with a general subscription to the things of God characteristic of all people of good will. I say this, not because I believe this accurately describes our current situation, but because it is a common complaint. On occasions when I have playfully asked students whether they would be willing to enlist in a temporary stint as a Christian missioner, they drew blanks; the only thing which came to mind was the religious education classes they had endured in grammar school and high school. None of them warmed to the idea of standing at a street corner, or on a milk crate in some metropolitan park, and shouting about Jesus. However, when they were asked about volunteering a year's service to assist the disadvantaged, they generally reacted not only positively, but also enthusiastically.

I do not wish for a minute to suggest that Christian literacy is unimportant, or that bearing witness to one's beliefs, even in the fashion of street-preaching evangelists, has no place among us. But one reason why young people initially draw a blank when this sort of prospect is proposed is that they do not know what they might possibly be able to say. Or to put the matter differently, they cannot find anything in their inventory of beliefs which they would want to stand up and shout about. To be sure, they share the North American attitude that one's religious beliefs are a personal matter; to preach them on a soap box would be to intrude on another's sacred space. Yet beyond this they find it very difficult to state any belief which is particularly exciting to them; even the belief they usually name first, that Jesus died to take away our sins, is offered more out of a sense of obligation to the tradition than from a sense of personal meaningfulness.

The uneasiness which my students showed when attempting to answer this question pointed me in the direction of wondering whether they might not actually be responding appropriately. The story of Jesus is more important to the Christian community itself than to the outside world. For us, hearing that story is what sustains and nourishes our faith, makes our faith subversive, and urges us toward mission. I could not conceive of sharing the riches of *Un tal Jesus*, for example, with people who are not members of the Christian community. Evangelization of the church itself is one thing; here we constantly renew ourselves by learning to read with fresh eyes the gospel story. This familiarity with the story of Jesus, furthermore, is the presupposition of truly adult religious literacy.

Telling the Story with Our Lives

But evangelization of those on the outside is something different. There we speak best, perhaps, by the words of our lives, since action and example are what testify most forcefully to the integrity of the faith we carry in our hearts. Whenever people on the outside ask me about what makes me the sort of person I am, I will readily answer "Jesus." But ordinarily I do not find myself drawn immediately to want to talk about the gospel story. Instead, I may begin talking about myself, my history, and the history of my faith. However many stories of Jesus we have, ultimately they are *Christian* stories, and I no more feel comfortable speaking to outsiders about them than I would be if I were telling them stories about my own family. Even then, I do not share personal family stories in order to attract people into letting us adopt them; but something like adoption is what I might have in mind in speaking to outsiders about things of faith. The Christian community shares its stories with men and women who want to become part of that community, because one cannot be part of a family without knowing the stories which brought and keep it together.

It is not an uncommon experience among those who work among poor and disadvantaged people with little or no religious faith that the interior reasons or spiritual motivation behind their efforts rarely come to the fore. Few people ask about the religious things that make us tick, except perhaps as a way of being courteous or polite. People are not easily drawn to converse openly and seriously about the things of God. Yet they do take individuals whom they see to be working selflessly among them with the utmost seriousness and respect. The story of Jesus, which means so much to me, hardly ever comes to expression in my dealings with people outside the community of believers. Yet that does not mean they are not hearing the story: they both hear and watch it implicitly through the practice of those who live for others, as Jesus did. Anyone who is passionately seeking the kingdom of God, who actively lives out God's own preferential love for the poor, and who wants nothing more than to be in the company of Jesus, is already telling the gospel story. The story of Jesus has become one's own; it is his life which is unfolding in and through ours. This is the most basic form of evangelization I can imagine.

The story which I would begin telling to outsiders probably would not be the story of Jesus; that would come later. Rather, I would start with the historical experience of the Christian community and the community's own stories. I would talk, for example, about the suffering and struggle of Christian communities in Central and South America today, since they form an integral part of the contemporary biography of faith. I would want to talk about the Christian community as the bearer of humanity's hope that the work of creation should one day be fulfilled. The community keeps alive humanity's trust in the divine promise, the very same promise which lies at the bottom of Jesus' own zealous dedication to the kingdom of God. For what makes the life of Jesus intelligible and compelling is his passionate devotion to the kingdom of God. Later, after the resurrection, when the early communities came to share and to preach the story of Jesus, the prominence of the kingdom appears to have receded. And once that happened, it was too easy to single out the identity of Jesus as the Son of God and humanity's "spiritual" savior as the most important element of its catechesis, together with the church as the place where salvation is offered. Yet these elements are clearly secondary. The identity of Jesus is more important to those inside the household of faith than to those outside. Whenever the content of the gospel is reduced to being a revelation of the miracle of the Word of God becoming flesh, the church will view its primary mission as that of proclaiming the presence of the incarnate Word in history, rather than proclaiming what was so central to the message of Jesus, namely, the imminence of the kingdom and God's making good on the divine promise to liberate human beings from all that has oppressed them.

For this reason, the Christian community's pursuit of justice and its tireless efforts to promote justice in the world (together with the faith upon which that concern rests, as it did for Jesus) become the basic form of evangelization to those outside. Once again, the identity of Jesus is a secondary issue; who he is is much more important to the believing community than it is to the world. And if the appearance of Jesus in our world testifies to God's great love for the human race, it does so precisely insofar as it confirms the divine desire to liberate and redeem men and women from all the sin, fear, poverty and injustice which makes their lives on earth miserable. First and last, the story of Jesus is always going to be good news for the poor (Lk 4:18), for the gospel means not only that God has elected to take their side in their struggle to overcome poverty and oppression; it also means that God has become actively involved in human affairs in order to alter the course of history. This is what the gospel is telling us. Furthermore, this liberating action is something which God continues to do in and through the community of disciples, who will be constantly nourished and enriched from retelling the story of Jesus.

A Select Bibliography

Leonardo Boff, *Jesus Christ Liberator* (Maryknoll: Orbis Books, 1978).
———, *Passion of Christ, Passion of the World* (Maryknoll: Orbis Books, 1987).
Raymond E. Brown, Joseph A. Fitzmyer and Roland E. Murphy, eds., *The New Jerome Biblical Commentary* (Englewood Cliffs, New Jersey: Prentice Hall, 1990).
Richard J. Cassidy, *Jesus, Politics and Society: A Study of Luke's Gospel* (Maryknoll: Orbis Books, 1978).
John Dominic Crossan, *The Historical Jesus: The Life of a Mediterranean Jewish Peasant* (San Francisco: HarperCollins, 1991).
John R. Donahue, *The Gospel as Parable* (Philadelphia: Fortress Press, 1988).
James D. G. Dunn, *Christology in the Making* (Philadelphia: Westminster Press, 1980).
———, *Jesus and the Spirit: A Study of the Religious and Charismatic Experience of Jesus and the First Christians as Reflected in the New Testament* (Philadelphia: Westminster Press, 1975).
———, *Jesus, Paul and the Law: Studies in Mark and Galatians* (Louisville: Westminster/John Knox Press, 1990).
Paula Fredriksen, *From Jesus to Christ: The Origin of the New Testament Images of Jesus* (New Haven: Yale University Press, 1988).
John P. Galvin, "Jesus Christ" in *Systematic Theology: Roman Catholic Perspectives*, 2 volumes, ed. Francis Schussler Fiorenza and John P. Galvin (Minneapolis: Fortress Press, 1991), I:249–324.
Kenneth Grayston, *Dying, We Live: A New Enquiry into the Death of Christ in the New Testament* (New York: Oxford University Press, 1990).

A. E. Harvey, *Jesus and the Constraints of History* (Philadelphia: Westminster Press, 1982).

Monika Hellwig, "Re-Emergence of the Human, Critical, Public Jesus," *Theological Studies* 50:3 (1989), 466–480.

Richard A. Horsley, *Jesus and the Spiral of Violence: Popular Jewish Resistance in Roman Palestine* (San Francisco: Harper & Row, 1987).

Marinus de Jonge, *Christology in Context: The Earliest Christian Response to Jesus* (Philadelphia: Westminster Press, 1988).

————, *Jesus, The Servant-Messiah* (New Haven: Yale University Press, 1991).

J. N. D. Kelly, *Early Christian Doctrines* (San Francisco: Harper & Row, 1959.

James P. Mackey, *Jesus: The Man and the Myth* (Mahwah, New Jersey: Paulist Press, 1979).

John P. Meier, *A Marginal Jew: Rethinking the Historical Jesus* (New York: Doubleday & Co., 1991).

Jürgen Moltmann, *The Way of Jesus Christ: Christology in Messianic Dimensions*, trans. Margaret Kohl (San Francisco: Harper Collins, 1990).

Frederick J. Murphy, *The Religious World of Jesus* (Nashville: Abingdon Press, 1991).

Gerald O'Collins, *Interpreting Jesus* (Mahwah, New Jersey: Paulist Press, 1983).

————, *Jesus Risen* (Mahwah, New Jersey: Paulist Press, 1987).

Karl Rahner, *The Foundations of Christian Faith* (New York: Seabury Press, 1978), 176–321.

John Riches, *Jesus and the Transformation of Judaism* (New York: Seabury Press, 1982).

Edward Schillebeeckx, *Jesus: An Experiment in Christology* (New York: Seabury Press, 1979).

————, *Christ: The Experience of Jesus as Lord* (New York: Seabury Press, 1980).

Juan Luis Segundo, *The Historical Jesus of the Synoptics* (Maryknoll: Orbis Books, 1985).

Jon Sobrino, *Christology at the Crossroads: A Latin American Approach* (Maryknoll: Orbis Books, 1978).

José Ignacio and María López Vigil, *Un tal Jesus: La Buena Noticia contada al pueblo de América Latina*, 2 volumes (Salamanca: Loguez Ediciones, 1982).

RECOMMENDED READING

Raymond Brown, *Responses to 101 Questions on the Bible* (Mahwah, New Jersey: Paulist Press, 1990).

Jose Miguez Bonino, ed., *Faces of Jesus: Latin American Christologies* (Maryknoll: Orbis Books, 1984).

Marcus J. Borg, *Jesus: A New Vision* (San Francisco: Harper & Row, 1987).

Bernard J. Cooke, *God's Beloved: Jesus' Experience of the Transcendent* (Philadelphia: Trinity Press International, 1992).

Joseph A. Fitzmyer, *A Christological Catechism: New Testament Answers* (Mahwah, New Jersey: Paulist Press, revised edition, 1991).

Monika Hellwig, *Jesus the Compassion of God* (Wilmington: Michael Glazier, 1983).

Elizabeth A. Johnson, *Consider Jesus: Waves of Renewal in Christology* (New York: Crossroad Publishing Co., 1990).

Dermot A. Lane, *The Reality of Jesus* (Mahwah, New Jersey: Paulist Press, 1975).

Albert Nolan, *Jesus Before Christianity* (Maryknoll: Orbis Books, 1978; revised edition, 1992).

Gerald O'Collins, *What Are They Saying About Jesus?* (Mahwah, New Jersey: Paulist Press, 1977).

Gerard S. Sloyan, *Jesus In Focus: A Life in its Setting* (Mystic, Conn.: Twenty-Third Publications, 1983).

———, *Jesus: Redeemer and Divine Word* (Wilmington: Michael Glazier, 1989).

C. S. Song, *Jesus, The Crucified People* (New York: Crossroad Publishing Co., 1990.)